AF230089

INCOME BLISS

INCOME BLISS

Create a Retirement Income
THAT YOU CAN'T *OUTLIVE*

BOB GARDNER,
CLU, ChFC, RFC

COPYRIGHT © 2020 BOB GARDNER

All rights reserved.

INCOME BLISS

Create a Retirement Income That You Can't Outlive

ISBN   978-1-5445-0938-9   *Paperback*
       978-1-5445-0939-6   *Ebook*

Dedicated to my family: To my wife Kat and our children, who have watched me stare vacantly over my laptop as I tried to weave actual client stories into a very sterile planning process, trying to add life to a more-often-than-not boring subject. Without their support, I would still be "hoping" to complete this book.

CONTENTS

PREFACE

Things can change—quickly! It has been my life's mission for the last ten years to help retirees create an income stream that lasts as long as they are on planet Earth. The hardest part of my profession is to encourage our clients to seek lifetime income versus investment growth during their retirement years.

I've been working on this book for a while. In fact, we were about to bring it to completion in December 2016 when my life changed dramatically—and I personally learned the importance of my own book's advice.

My wife and I had planned a Disney World Christmas for our large family (four children, two spouses, four grandchildren, and two Labrador retrievers!). We were all excited, especially the grandkids, and were leaving for Orlando on Sunday morning, December 18. Things do not always follow our plans.

Around 9:30 p.m. on December 17, my wife and I were in the final throes of packing for the trip. (That means that my wife was packing as I watched a nondescript football game while stretched out on our bed.) Kat, my wife, headed into the kitchen to pack the things our dogs needed, while I volunteered to continue watching the game. Walking out of the bedroom, as she has done hundreds of times with me snoring in the background, she turned to see me in what appeared to be a seizure. I was not breathing, my eyes were open, and my fists were clenched under my chin. After failing to wake me, Kat called 911. Praise the Lord, they arrived at our home in less than five minutes. The next thing I knew, I woke up in an ambulance with three paramedics staring down at me, and I had no clue how I had arrived there.

I had suffered something called ventricular fibrillation. Most times, it's fatal, but thanks to my wife and the awesome EMT team—particularly Dominic Sose, who was subbing for someone else (divine intervention?)—I am here to tell the tale and finish my book. I am also the proud owner of a pacemaker and defibrillator in the left side of my chest, and I could not be happier to sport this new accessory to my wardrobe. The great thing is that this particular event will never happen again thanks to this new technology.

The point of my story is this: take care of your income and legacy planning while you are upright and healthy. Unlike me, you may not get a second chance.

STEADY AT THE HELM

Dennis came to see me after attending one of my seminars in 2006. In hindsight, I don't know why he even bothered. After all, he had already almost made up his mind to go with one of the big wealth management shops. Who could blame him? It's not every day you get 10 percent returns.

Back in those days, promising someone a 10 percent return was not uncommon. The big shops did it all the time, and some of them still do. In Dennis's case, that amounted to $400,000 per year on $4 million—nothing to sniff at.

There's only one problem with 10 percent returns: they don't happen. At least not on an annualized basis.

Dennis was sixty-six years old at the time, still working. He came to see me and said, "Bob, I've got $4 million, but I need to start thinking about income for retirement."

I told him that anyone who promises 10 percent returns knows something I don't. And after being in this business for more than three decades, there is not much I do not know when it comes to planning for retirement.

I explained that a more cautious approach, one that still provides income and liquidity for life, was the best model to follow. That fell on deaf ears. I told him that at his age, he was taking on too much market risk, playing with fire—he did not share my assessment.

We shook hands, and Dennis took his money to the big shop of 10 percent returns. Fast-forward to 2010. The phone rings. It's Dennis.

"Bob, this is Dennis. Do you remember me?"

"Oh, boy," I said. "Yes, I do. Why are you calling?"

"Well, I have to tell you what happened," he said. "I stayed in the market. I lost and kept losing. I sold on the lowest day of the year in March 2009."

"I am sorry to hear that," I said.

"Long story short," he said, "my $4 million became $1.6 million."

We all know what the Great Recession did to the markets. Dennis, unfortunately, learned the hard way.

"My hair was falling out. My wife wouldn't speak to me. I couldn't sleep at night. And to make matters worse, I have not been back in the market."

Because he had taken too much risk early on, Dennis missed the rest of 2009, which finished 20 percent up. He had been financially paralyzed while other investors recouped some of their losses.

"I tried to do some of the things you showed me at your seminar," he said. "I've read books on retirement and investing, but I just can't figure it out."

I had a feeling Dennis was trying to ask me something.

"I cannot run out of money. I have to make it last. If I bring you my $1.6 million, can you help?"

Over the years, I have learned how important client relationships are. Sometimes, I am not the right fit for a client. Maybe it's my forthcoming personality or the way I recommend managing money. Other times, a client might not be the right fit for me. He or she does not want to listen to my recommendations, or needs total control, or enjoys taking on too much risk. Whatever the reason, it's imperative that clients and I see eye to eye. I was pretty sure Dennis and I did not, but I was trying to grow my business. Against my better judgment, I said yes.

"Here's the deal," I said. "If you are serious about working together, and meet with me next week, I will put together a retirement plan for you. I will do the research, the hard work, and present you with a plan that will provide you with income for life. But you must pledge to implement my suggestions and stay the course. Are you okay with that?"

"Yes," he said.

"And Dennis, if I do this for you, and then you try to take the plan and do it yourself, or bring it to another advisor, well, Dennis, then I will be furious. You and I will not be friends. Are you okay with that?"

"Yep," he said.

I did not think he would come to the meeting. But lo and behold, I was wrong. It turns out that Dennis was acquainted with a pair of my clients, a husband and wife. They were golfing together one day, and Dennis asked them about their advisor. When they told Dennis that Bob Gardner managed their money, Dennis was surprised.

"We like Bob because he keeps our money safe," they told him. And with that referral, I had a new client.

This is not an "I told you so" story, but rather a way to illustrate the importance of professional guidance. Dennis has been with me for more than five years now. He is a solid client. But if he had become a client in 2006, we would not need to push the envelope to meet his income needs today. Every client has his needs, and ultimately, it's his money, so he can do with it what he wants. But Dennis lost a considerable amount in the market, and now at seventy-two, he is still working.

High-risk investments are alluring and can deliver outstanding returns, but it only takes one good bear market to decimate all the money you have grown. If you are near retirement, that type of risk is simply too much. I tell people that investing is like running a marathon. If you run twenty-six miles but do not prepare for the last 385 yards, you might as well stay in bed. What's more, if you have been a diligent money saver and have reasonable lifestyle expectations, you do not need to earn vast sums of money to live wonderfully. All you have to do is manage risk and avoid severe losses. You do that by adhering to a plan that measures growth and safety in equal measure; it is called the "Income Bliss" model.

This book hinges on a single question: "How can I make sure I will have enough money to last the rest of my life and beyond?"

Most people do not ask this question, and if they do, they do not calculate an honest answer. Why? Because it's too sobering. It's too real. It reflects a primal fear that surfaces no matter if you live from paycheck to paycheck or have millions in the bank. It's a question that highlights the need for careful planning.

Make no mistake about it, retirement is a new phase of life and the rules have changed. The focus is no longer on accumulating money, but on protecting it. Retirees are in peril if they fail to adjust to this new reality. I try to get the message to people as early as possible. If you haven't saved money for the forty years of your working life, no investment advisor, including me, can pull a rabbit out of the hat and make everything all right. Bad planning by you does not constitute an emergency on my part. Diligent planning allows you to make money slowly, and slowly making money is the only way that is predictable and avoids risk.

We can minimize risk, but every financial decision still has an associated opportunity cost. In Dennis's case, he paid an enormous opportunity cost by losing money in the market, and because he did not take advantage of the market's eventual rebound. Most people, however, have not even heard about opportunity cost, let alone thought about it.

Put simply, opportunity cost states that every time you use a dollar, for whatever reason, you give up the chance to use that dollar somewhere else. Opportunity cost is a concept we will frequently visit in this book. It is a key to financial success and should be central to every decision.

If you take everything you know about the financial advice industry, whether it's information from stockbrokers, financial planners, insurance people, or even Jim Cramer, the thread that stitches all of it together is hype. Everything in this industry is built on hype. If one big shop can get you 10 percent returns, some other big shop can get you 12 percent, another one can get you 14 percent, and so on.

Here is an example: twenty-five years ago, when I didn't have two nickels to rub together, a stockbroker called me. He called me because my name was on a list that said I'd purchased or was interested in buying stocks. Here's how the conversation went:

"Hello, Bob. How are you today? If I could show you a way to make 10 percent, 12 percent, 14 percent in the next three months, how much money could you devote to this investment today?"

"Well, I don't think any," I said.

"Well, how much do you have to invest?" he asked.

"Zero," I said.

The next sound I heard was the dial tone. This guy was not interested in trying to help me find money to invest. He was merely saying, "Invest with us. We have a better mousetrap. Whatever the other guys said they could get, we can get more."

Unfortunately, this is the crux on which our entire industry is predicated. Nobody can get these high returns with any certainty, but promising them to new investors is the easiest and fastest thing a stockbroker can do to try to get his next commission check. Part of the biggest problem in the industry, from an advisor's point of view, is the need to sell something every day. To sell something, you have to free up capital, and that's not always to the benefit of the client. Opportunity cost comes into play in this scenario, and I always make decisions based on the best way to deploy a dollar, not because we need to free up capital.

We will not promise 10 percent returns next year, because our goal is to provide you with income for life. Everything we do is based on math and is provable. If you are reading this looking for the highest return possible, I suggest you close the book and turn out the light. Investment advice is not this book's purpose, since proper investment advice depends on an individual's circumstances, needs, and goals. If you are a thrill seeker who, over a game of golf, wants to brag about or lament how your investments have performed, this book is not for you.

This book is for those who wish to ride the market higher, but only with that portion of their money they can afford to dedicate to that purpose. This book is for those who understand the importance of knowing their purpose and goals in life. Before risking anything, though, they make sure they have covered their short-term needs and will have an income to last a lifetime.

WHO WE ARE

WSG Partners LLC and WSG Advisors LLC are privately held financial services firms based in Hilton Head Island, South Carolina, with one satellite office in Greenville, South Carolina. Since founding our company in 1981, we've evolved into a full-service financial, investment, and estate planning organization offering comprehensive financial advice and services to individuals and corporations. While the majority of our clients are retirees and individuals close to retirement, with the addition of new, younger talent to our team, we are now offering our planning knowledge to a new demographic, including young professionals, families with college-bound children, and growing businesses. That said, we are not for everyone. Our philosophy, principles, and approach differentiate us from others in our industry.

The first tenet of our business is trust. Our clients trust us with their money. We understand that, ultimately, the client makes the final decision, and we trust them to implement the suggestions we provide. Those suggestions are never dramatic. In fact, they are boring. And I say that with pride. We make money slowly, over time, and believe in winning by not losing. If you have done a decent job of saving money, it is entirely possible to have a great retirement without taking unnecessary risks. If you are looking to beat the market, you are on the wrong team.

We adhere so strictly to our principles and philosophy because they help build the foundation for the entire planning process. We design each client's financial plan up-front and expect allegiance to it. We are not looking for clients who zig when we say zag. After all, the client is fully aware of the plan's machinations—nothing is a surprise—and allegiance to it is essential to its overall success. If we are in a bull market, some clients may get excited and want to chart a new course. That is wrong. Since we ride the market for the long term, each plan is built in anticipation of the market's fluctuations. If we are in a bear market, and others are watching their money disappear, our clients are protected and sleep well at night.

That said, even after we have a plan ready to implement, we remain proactive yet patient in our approach. When things turn bad, we are not hiding on the sidelines. We regularly monitor each client's situation and contact him or her to consult on the next best moves. And because we are consistent in our approach, because we are resolute in our philosophy, our clients know in advance the type of advice we provide. In fact, due to this provision of consistency in our philosophy, we typically turn away more people than we accept. Our primary job is to protect a client's assets while keeping them from going broke. If that does not gel with their goals, we do not need to be in business together. In short, we pick our clients as much as they pick us.

As I have mentioned, and will again throughout this book, each and every retirement income plan we devise is designed to provide the client with income for the rest of his or her life, and beyond. To achieve this, we tailor plans for the individual. Each has unique goals, values, risk tolerance, and a portfolio of assets that may or may not be realistic for retirement. To be successful, to design a custom plan that does as much as possible, we must get to know our clients. We talk to them. We learn their age, their level of income and wealth, their career history, their outlook on life and retirement.

Most often, we work with people age fifty-five and older who are anticipating retirement or who have already entered it. My clientele typically has minimum net investable assets of $750,000 to about $5 million, but the average is usually between $1.5 and $3 million. It has been a long journey since I first started in the insurance industry more than thirty years ago. For the first five or six years, I did not make any money. I just had to stick it out. But that's what it takes to succeed in this business—long-term goals.

I didn't always think about long-term goals or financial advice. In fact, once upon a time, I wanted to be a musician. For a brief period, I was traveling with a rock 'n' roll band and playing at different bars and clubs across the country. I enjoyed playing my guitar in front of an audience, the rush of standing up there, but I could read the writing on the wall. It was time for me to grow up. I needed a real job.

I entered the insurance industry as an agent in 1981. Two years later, I was a midline manager at American General Group in Charlotte, North Carolina. That's when I started taking the work seriously. But I would still get calls from my old bandmates, asking me to fill in for a guitar player who couldn't do a gig. I considered it. It called to me, but I didn't answer.

I stayed in the business and won the battle of attrition. Most guys don't stay. That's why we have a 90 percent failure rate in this business—because people can't make it long enough to succeed. There are also plenty of agents out there who never become true professionals simply because they were not trained properly. Remember, amateurs teach amateurs to be amateurs. Somehow, though, by the grace of God and because I had good mentors, over time, I made it.

I left American General in 1985 for American Bankers and climbed the corporate ladder to regional vice president and later, director of agencies. I had a very successful run there, but ultimately, I knew I wanted to help people plan for retirement, not just sell them investments. But I didn't have the proper way of doing it. That's when I formed Wealth Strategies Group, which in time split into two entities: WSG Advisors and WSG Partners. At WSG, I have the opportunity to help people. Before, it was all about selling products. Now, I help clients plan for what truly can be a special time in their lives. I even joke with my friends in the ministry and friends who are doctors that I help my clients more than they do, and as a result of our work, they stay healthy and have more time and money to support their local churches or other worthy charities. They don't always agree with me, of course.

Now that I have given some details on my background and experience, and laid out an overview of my philosophy, values, and approach to retirement planning, let's look forward to the chapters ahead and see what the "Income Bliss" model is all about. In the following chapters, readers will:

- Learn how to breathe freely with an income plan designed to make sure there is enough income to last a lifetime.

- Get a close look at the Social Security system: Will the benefit still be there for future retirees? When should retirees take it?

- Learn how pensions have given way to 401(k)s, and the implications for planning for retirement.

- Receive general advice on finding a good advisor and the importance of teamwork.

- Learn about inflation, taxes, hidden fees in mutual funds, healthcare, long-term care costs, and other threats to one's wealth—in short, the issues that weigh on retirees' minds.

- Receive the promise of moving forward with confidence, free of debilitating fear, to make the most of life savings— plus some essential practical advice on legacy, charitable giving, and estate planning.

* Learn how to manage risk—balancing the need to protect life savings with the need to grow assets to beat inflation and share the bounty with generations to come.

* Learn how to recover all costs associated with cars and major purchases and how to select the correct mortgage for you and your loved ones.

CHAPTER 1

WHO CHANGED THE RULES?

THE GOAL OF THIS BOOK IS TO EXPLAIN HOW RETIRE-ment works, to help people prepare and acknowledge the challenges ahead. With guidance, retirement can be a delightful and fruitful period. However, if you do not plan diligently, or if you have unrealistic expectations, retirement can be hard. My job is to make sure that every single client is set up for a successful retirement, and that there is enough income to last for life, and beyond.

This chapter focuses on what current retirees or those retiring soon should understand as they enter a new phase in life.

First, retirement may very well not be what you expect—regarding how you spend your money and where that money comes from—and it's essential that you adjust to this reality as soon as possible.

When a client understands this approach and philosophy and is determined to make money slowly and to keep it safe, it's off into the sunset we go. Everything is great. On the other hand, if a client is stubborn, or wants to beat the market for huge returns, well, then we have problems. The first problem is that huge returns are unpredictable and inconsistent. Retirement is not the time to gamble assets. The second problem is that even if I could deliver 12 percent returns within a couple of years, I would not do it. Investing with that type of risk goes against my principles and shortchanges the client from receiving what I can promise: income for life.

Ultimately, it all comes down to the client. After three decades in this business, I can usually tell within minutes if someone is the right fit. The ability to do so saves time and pain—for them and me. Occasionally, though, I'll have a client who at first blush seems like a fit, but then will throw a curveball and everything changes. Take John and Katherine.

John and Katherine lived on John's very high income of more than $400,000 per year. They had a wealthy lifestyle but poor saving habits. John was still working when they first came to see me. Up to that point, though, they'd only saved about

$500,000. So, we had a couple nearing retirement who were used to an extravagant lifestyle—international travel, homes, cars, and so on—and wanted to make retirement an extension of their current experience. "Bob," they said, "make it work."

The only way to make it work, in this case, is to deliver 8 to 10 percent in bad times and 12 to 14 percent in good times. Here's the hard truth: you can't do it. John and Katherine did not plan for retirement properly, and now they were going to have to make sacrifices. That is not what they wanted to hear.

When they first came to see me, about two years before John was slated to retire, and I examined their assets and discussed their goals and values, they told me they were amenable to cutting their income. If that's what needed to happen to provide them with income for life, so be it. Besides, they said, in the future, they would not want to travel the way they did now; they would not care for the finer things in life the way they did now.

A funny thing happened as John's retirement neared.

Suddenly, the reality that their income was about to drop dramatically hit home, and they panicked. They were looking for someone to blame. They told me again, "We don't want to travel later in life, and we don't have to be so conservative with our assets. We want our money to grow now."

That's when I knew we had problems. I spoke to John. He never accused me of doing anything wrong or managing his money poorly. He thought I was just too conservative. "You're right," I said. "I am. I do not want to be a part of your running out of money. At this rate, that's what is going to happen."

I told him he had two options: lower his income expectations, or hope that he died quickly. Harsh as that might sound, it was true. There simply was not enough money to provide income for life while meeting his and Katherine's lifestyle goals. He could reevaluate these objectives to match the reality of his income, or he could go ahead and die, in which case he would not, in fact, run out of money. Well, John and I agreed to disagree. Shortly thereafter, we referred him and Katherine to another advisor.

This story provides a valuable lesson for multiple reasons. First, it illustrates the pitfalls of not planning carefully for your retirement years, even if you are coming from a high-income background. Second, it highlights how people change their minds when reality sets in and money is not available. I never like losing a client, but in this case, it was better for John and Katherine to find an advisor who was willing to take significant risks. And it was better for me, too. As I told John, I did not want to be a part of his running out of money, the ultimate failure. That holds true for all my clients.

Which brings us to the point I made about adjusting expectations about retirement.

New retirees usually want to sit back, enjoy their new freedom, and watch the sunset. But after a little while, as they are sitting there not doing much, they look at each other and say, "God, this is boring." Very soon, they'll most likely start doing something else. Where I live, in Hilton Head, South Carolina, a lot of retirees play golf. Some of them play five, six, seven days a week. That's a lot of golf, and I say that as someone who loves the game.

I like to play and am a decent golfer, but after playing a couple of days in a single week, I don't want to see that course again, ever. In 2010, I went to Scotland on a dream trip with some friends and my brother. We played six courses in six days. It was wonderful, don't get me wrong—I am 100 percent Scottish—but I was tired, drained, and I was sick of golf.

Some people, however, can do it. They fill their days with one activity, and it is enough. Other people need to do something else, to branch out. It's all part of learning about who you are and want to be in this new experiment called retirement. Some people volunteer and give back to the community. Others find a different hobby or interest. But most everyone quickly realizes that some kind of engaging activity needs to fill this new phase.

Occasionally, if a recent retiree has not given it much thought, this new phase can be troubling. The first thing to go is your work identity, a role you have played for decades, and with that goes your regular paycheck. That can put a strain on a marriage. When you are retired, you spend much more time with your spouse. So, it is vital that new retirees discuss individual and mutual goals, dreams, and values. Discuss how to spend the days. Will you visit the grandkids or enjoy rocking chairs on the porch? Some retirees like to stay busy with trips and entertainment, and, in turn, spend more than they can afford. There is no single solution for each. The more time spent discussing and planning for retirement, the better. A great plan, customized for an individual's retirement, goes a long way to ensuring peace of mind and happiness. If I were a betting man, I'd wager John and Katherine face some hard decisions in the near future. The longer you delay, the harder it is to design a retirement plan that coincides with your expectations.

Sometimes it can feel as if the rules of life have changed. The things you used to worry about—starting a family, buying a house, raising children, saving for college, perhaps paying off an increasing debt load—are gone and replaced by new worries. During your career years, it's okay to focus on advancing professionally and elevating your lifestyle. And in those days, because your biggest asset was time, you could afford to invest aggressively, to take on risk. But everything changes in retirement. It is the preservation stage of life.

Strategies used in the accumulation phase of your career years may prove counterproductive now—for example, saving money. The dollar-cost average is a legitimate way to save money during the years you bring home a salary. That means that each month you buy a certain number of shares or put a fixed amount of money in the bank or purchase multiple mutual funds. Each month, you buy the investment at a different price, but over time, the price averages out. So, you accumulate money across years. When you are in the retirement phase, this approach is counterproductive, because you end up pulling money from a portfolio that requires a certain amount of stabilized capital to be useful. A 100 percent stock portfolio when you are thirty-five is fine, because you can endure four or five large corrections—because you're not taking money out. In retirement, you do not have that luxury. You have to protect your assets.

Accumulating money is relatively straightforward; you have to save it, of course, but investing in various ways that bring decent returns over time is fairly simple. Markets go up, and markets go down, but it's still a victory because of the dollar-cost average. So, even if you have a major setback, you can emerge relatively unscathed because there is still time. Time is your friend when it comes to investing. But in retirement, there is not so much time left, and you can't always win back what you lose. There are no do-overs in retirement.

I mention this to drive the point home that retirement is a new phase requiring a new approach.

A good analogy is climbing Mount Everest. What is the goal of scaling the tallest peak on the planet? Most people would say,

"To get to the top." While that is true, getting down would be more important to me. You may or may not know that well over half the fatalities happen on the descent from scaling Mount Everest. Let's apply this to financial planning: any number of financial planners, stockbrokers, insurance agents, etc., can get you up the mountain, primarily because you have "do-over" time to replace lost funds and double-down on saving. Not so in retirement. Retirement is the ultimate descent from the top of the mountain. If you're hiring a guide—a Sherpa—wouldn't it make sense to hire the professional who has the best record for getting people down the mountain safely? If you answer yes, then firms like mine are a good fit and will serve you well. If you are interested only in getting to the top, well, you can expend all your energy, food, and luck on the way up and pray vigorously on the way down.

Retirement, when properly planned for, is a tranquil, happy period. But it is not without its concerns. Chief among them, of course, is running out of money. That can happen in a number of ways. If you are carrying too much risk by investing a disproportionate amount in the market, what happens when the market trends down? You lose a disproportionate amount. Suddenly you are out of money, and your number-one concern is a reality. I've stressed this before, and will again throughout this book, but the retiree interested in beating the market for huge returns does not belong in my office.

The next significant worry is taxes. Taxes continue to be one of the driving forces in retirement planning, and paying too much each year is a major roadblock to success. A sound retirement plan executes under the assumption that taxes will continue to increase but one should do everything possible, within reason, to avoid paying overmuch. With enough time and cooperation, we can help you lower or even eliminate taxes on your retirement income under the right conditions.

Additional financial concerns, which reinforce the need for income and liquidity, include the following:

- Losing assets in the event of a nursing home stay or lawsuit
- Not having money readily available in the event of an emergency
- Government, not heirs, receiving the lion's share of your estate
- Planning for children or grandchildren
- Losing ground to inflation

These are all reasonable concerns, and we have ways of making strides against them. Regarding inflation, it is my job to ensure that a client's money is earning at least as much as inflation. And while we cannot control the inflation rate, we can be prepared for an increased rate so your assets are not hijacked.

Despite everything you may know about retirement, your best-laid plans are at risk of being diverted or wrecked by a variety of threats, including illness, a stock market crash, emergencies, the death of a spouse, or divorce. A good advisor prepares you to weather these storms.

After all, you need only three things to succeed in retirement:

1. Income: you need sufficient cash flow to support your lifestyle, replacing that paycheck from your career years.

2. Liquidity: available money for the things you need to pay for, whether it's a new car, a wedding, or a medical emergency.

3. Legacy: everything else is your legacy, what you leave behind—whether it is for your children, a charity, your university, or your community.

When I prepare a retirement plan, I divide a client's assets into these three "buckets." The challenge is to figure out the proportions. But rest assured, everything you can dream up, no matter what it might be, fits into one of these buckets. My job is providing you with income for life and utilizing the rest of your assets in such a way so as to maximize the potential returns for years to come.

At this point in the book, we have a cursory understanding of what a fruitful and meaningful retirement plan resembles. We have reviewed a cautionary tale that illuminates the importance of saving and understanding what is required once you no longer have a salary to provide income. We have discussed how drastically life changes once you settle into retirement, and how important it is to focus on who you want to be during this new phase of your life. And we have considered some of the investing tactics that may have worked in the past but do not make sense when using an "Income Bliss" model.[1] Most important, we now understand that all of your assets go into one of three buckets: income, liquidity, and legacy.

I hope you are beginning to gain a clear picture of what it takes to make your retirement as peaceful and financially sound as possible. As I said at the beginning of this chapter, my goal is to help people plan for the future. Retirement planning is not something most people enjoy doing, but once it is clear that retirement planning is the same thing as life planning, the task grows closer to the heart. It is a plan we want to make right—a plan we must make right.

In closing, I'd like to say you are not alone. You are not alone in your concern; your feeling of stress or intimidation is not

---

1   The Income Bliss Model is a registered trademark of Wealth2k, Inc. Used by permission. Copyright 2004-2016 Wealth2k, Inc. All rights reserved.

exclusive to your experience. Many people, though they work their entire lives to get to it, are afraid of retirement. It does not have to be that way. My business is to take these various strategies and boil them down to their essential ingredients. I am not going to blather on about overly complicated topics that do not mean much to my clients. I am going to talk about what matters to them—kids, sports, politics, church, whatever. A client needs to trust his advisor. An advisor needs to believe and understand his clients. Combined with the assurance of a sound financial plan, the retirement phase of life does not have to be lived under restrictions. In fact, it can be liberating.

I work very hard for my clients. There is not a company on this planet that does a better job for the client after they become a client. That may be one of my strongest statements, but it is true. I love helping my clients, and I am determined to see them reap the rewards of all their hard work.

Earlier, we talked about the fear of retirement and some of the most common, inherent worries. I share those concerns, and in business, I have fears of my own. One of my biggest fears is that a client, someone who has been working with me for five or six years, will come up to me and say, "You know, Bob. If I knew then what I know now, I never would have worked with you."

That's my biggest fear in business because it means we steered a client in the wrong direction—that we did not do the math right or our suggestions were blind to risks. But I can proudly say that not once in more than three decades of business has that happened. I have not let it happen. Nor will I let it happen in the future.

CHAPTER 2

WHAT'S THE POINT OF YOUR MONEY?

ONEY IS JUST MONEY, A TOOL, UNLESS YOU KNOW what to do with it. Once you decide what your goals are, how you would like to put your resources to use, that is when money gains real importance and meaning. Of course, practically speaking, money is always important. We all have bills to pay. But in the retirement phase of life, your resources can lead you toward meaningful life goals, and understanding how to make that happen, planning for it, is tremendously important.

As we saw in the last chapter, when retirees do not have a grasp on the reality of their financial situation, when their lifestyle expectations do not line up with the capital they have at their disposal, it poses difficult questions. Like John and Katherine, when most people realize that the money they have saved does not permit the lifestyle they had envisioned, they look for advisors who promise preposterously high returns quickly. By now, we all know that high returns do not arrive with the consistency and predictability needed to achieve income for life.

In this chapter, we will cover the critical need to set priorities and goals for the rest of your life. We will examine how to plan effectively and realistically for the retirement phase. We will explore what it means to allocate funds for your legacy, and how to budget income for the first five to ten years of retirement, when most people remain active and spending, versus the subsequent ten years, when people tend to slow down and spend less. We will go into detail about how my firm conducts meetings, and how we decide to take on new clients. Finally, we will look at ways to organize important documents, who should have access to them, and why.

Overall, my goal for this chapter is to provide practical advice on how to prepare for retirement—beginning with the end in mind. That sounds easy, but it is not. Most people hear the word "end" and shirk away. Responsible retirees understand that "end" is not a dirty word. In fact, if a happy and prosperous retirement is the goal, beginning with the end in mind is the only way to approach the task.

We all have unrealistic expectations. In my younger days, playing guitar, I expected to be in a band, to be successful, to live that type of life. But with a wife and two young kids, it was unrealistic. I am so grateful that I learned that lesson while I was still young. It's served me my entire life and has informed the way I help clients prepare for retirement. Unrealistic expectations in retirement are somewhat different, though. That's because in retirement, everything you do—from how you spend your days to how you spend your money—must be firmly grounded in reality.

When we're young, it is easy to have unrealistic expectations because we have time and believe we can still achieve them. Not so in the retirement phase. As we all know, this stage is about preserving assets and earning money slowly and safely.

It is hard to identify what is realistic and what is not when it comes to retirement spending. Retirement does not mean the time for dreaming is over; it means there is time for dreaming, only with a fixed income. But how can you say with certainty what is realistic and what is unrealistic? Frankly, most people, when the market is up, are happy, and when the market is down, they're not. But that does not totally get to our point. One way to help clients decide what's realistic is to ask them about their goals. We don't focus on rates or returns, but rather on what they need to meet their objectives. What are their goals? How do they want to spend their money? These are the questions we can start to answer as soon as we divide assets up into income, liquidity, and legacy. When we identify those buckets and look at the income available, we then can begin addressing a client's goals. That is when the difference between real and unrealistic expectations becomes apparent. Of course, we never tell people how to live their lives—a client's money is her money. But under our "Income Bliss" model, some expectations can change. That's why it is so important to discuss goals, values, and expectations as early as possible, and to have a clear understanding of how your assets fit into the three buckets of income, liquidity, and legacy.

The first and most fundamental thing we do is to make sure every client has enough income to enjoy the rest of his or her life. Next, we make sure there is enough capital in the liquidity bucket. The liquidity bucket contains assets for things you either need or want, such as paying for your daughter's wedding, or going on a cruise, and so on. I've seen some interesting ways people budget for these things. Some want to plan them into their income; others don't budget for them at all. That's why we suggest that such expenses belong in the liquidity bucket. Things you want or need, outside of everyday items like eating and keeping a roof over your head, belong in the liquidity bucket.

To drive home this point, I often tell clients my air conditioner story. I bought a new home in Hilton Head in 2004. The home has three air-conditioning systems, two downstairs and one upstairs. I had never lived near saltwater, and so I didn't realize that it is rare for an air-conditioning unit to last twelve years. The heat and salt just eat away at the units. It's corrosive. So, a couple of summers back, the air conditioners were not performing well. We needed to replace them. We spent nearly $50,000 on new air-conditioning units. I was shocked. I was still working, so that helped. But in retirement, when you do not have a salary coming in, spending that kind of money on air-conditioning units is the last thing you want to do. And yet, everybody has a story like mine. The trick is to prepare. Identify the assets required for things you want or need to pay for and place them in the liquidity bucket.

The final bucket is for your legacy. We all know social capital is paramount in our culture. Well, after you have enough income for life, and we account for your wants and needs in the liquidity bucket, what is left? That is what we put in the legacy bucket. A legacy is what you leave behind. It accounts for how people know who you were and what you did with your time on planet Earth.

Remember, money is just money, a tool, until you know what you want to do with it. You must plan first and invest second. Until you identify your goals and priorities, you will not be able to create an effective retirement plan. You can't plan until you know what you want to do. An effective retirement plan is tailored to your particular needs and goals. I see my role as helping people make a plan and follow it.

Here are some questions you can ask yourself to help you get started:

- What are your dreams and goals? Write them down as a distinct part of your plan.
- What is important to you?
- Who is important to you?
- Whom do you wish to help?
- What do you want to learn?
- Where do you want to go?
- What makes you happy or fulfilled?
- What have you always wished you had time to do?
- What is on your "bucket list?"

The truth is that most retirees spend more in the first five years, and then slow down. So, what are the implications of that for planning purposes? It's crucial in the first five years to allocate enough for liquidity. We do that by adjusting the income and legacy buckets. If you want to take two trips per year for the first five years of retirement, that's terrific, but that money needs to come from somewhere. We make sure those funds are accessible and ideally placed, so they earn more than inflation. The name of the game is protection, preservation, and income. We protect what you have, preserve, and earn on those assets.

To go back to a concept we touched on in Chapter 1, retirement is a new phase of life. Some retirees wind up spending more in their early retirement than they did when they were still in their career years earning a paycheck. Others reduce their spending because they don't want to run out of money. The idea is to strike a balance while ensuring you live the type of life you want.

MEETINGS

In the first meeting with a potential client, we try to get to know them better. We attempt to determine if we can be of service to them. Do their assets warrant a retirement plan? Do they want our help? It sounds obvious that they would want our help, but it happens all the time that people come to see us, ask us for guidance, and then do not want it. Some people are used to being in charge, and they bristle when I put together a plan for them and try to be their retirement coach. They need too much control and second-guess every decision I make. From a client's standpoint, it is essential to realize early on—and we never shy away from explaining this—that they must be comfortable working with an advisory firm that is realistic, that is not going to promise 12 percent and 15 percent returns.

Some people take umbrage when we tell them we won't deliver 12 percent. They say Jim Cramer and Suze Orman on television claim it is easy to make 12 percent or 14 percent on mutual funds. The problem is it's simply not true. Here's a secret: when you're not a certified advisor, but just some talking head on television, you can say anything you want. You can get away with murder.

During the first meeting, the potential client provides us with an overview of their assets. If the assets appear to be within the range in which we typically work, and the potential client does not lead us to believe he is a performance junkie out to topple the market, we schedule a second meeting. People are good at acting, though. And over the years, I have learned that it is just as important for me to evaluate the new client as it is for him to evaluate me. Some people come in, ask dozens of questions to elicit as much information as possible, and then try to take that information and apply it. They try to do retirement planning on their own. Well, that wastes my time, and it takes advantage of my generosity. That is why I had to sharpen my detection skills early on, so I could see as soon as possible if a person was a right fit for me.

The do-it-yourself mentality is pervasive in retirement planning. Typically, when a person makes a meeting only to glean information from me, what happens is I begin asking questions, such as these:

- "What are your goals for your money?"
- "Are those goals interest-rate driven, or earnings driven?"
- "Do you want to make sure you can pay all your bills, enjoy retirement, and not worry about running out of money?"

If I ask these questions, and they shoot me a pained look, I know they probably have an ulterior motive. If they then say, "I've got this stock, what do you think about it?" Well, that's the kiss of death. We're not going to work together.

I say, "Look, we're not a good fit. You just want someone to give advice and affirmation for what you've done. I am here to help you plan, not give stock advice."

That doesn't happen all the time, fortunately, but it does happen. I mention it here to ward off any would-be do-it-your-self investors.

More often, I meet with people who genuinely need help planning their financial futures. In most cases, I begin by asking, "Do you mind if I lay out this meeting?"

Maybe this helps, maybe it doesn't. But I have never had anyone say no. Usually, they say, "Hey, that would be great." Or, "Yes, please do. I don't know what to expect."

Then I say, "Well, how much time do you have?"

I do this right away, because if someone only has half an hour, I need to compress the meeting, not let it run for two hours. Regardless of how much time they have, I say, "Today, we're going to determine one thing. We are going to determine if we are going to have a second meeting."

We discover that by asking questions. Does our expertise lend to what they are trying to accomplish? Will they allow us to help? These are important details. Sometimes people can get in their own way, and they make decisions at a pace a turtle could outrun. We can't work like that. A good client trusts us to provide them with timely and vetted suggestions. I don't want any mystification in the process. I ask them, "If there is one thing that we could accomplish today to make your trip to my office worthwhile, what would it be?"

Often, people meet with us because they have attended one of my seminars or classes, which I put on regularly. Maybe they are losing money, or are dissatisfied with their stockbroker, or feel they are paying too much in taxes. People who come to my seminars respond to our "Income Bliss" model. "That sounds good," they say. They want to learn more.

I ask questions, trying to get at the heart of the matter: Should we do business together?

- "How much money do you have in the bank?"
- "How much money do you have in the market?"
- "How much money do you have in IRAS?"
- "Which individual stocks do you own?"

- "Do you have any brokerage accounts?"
- "How much real estate or property do you own?"
- "Do you own or are you a partner in any businesses?"
- "Do you have a pension?"
- "What do you have in Social Security?"

Once we move through these questions, establishing an income floor, I ask them to tell me about their personal lives, kids, grandkids—how many?

Accumulated, the answers to these questions provide a composite glimpse at the potential client. If they want me to put a plan together based on the information provided, I say, "Terrific. Let's do that." But plans, even preliminary ones, take time. So now we need to set the second meeting. Before we schedule a second meeting, I need to know for sure that the prospect wants to work with us. I ask directly, "Do you wish to be a client?" If they pause and say they need time to consider, I ask how much time. If they cannot answer, I take it as a no. If they say, "Gosh, it will take a month for me to make that decision"—well, I think that's untrue. That's just a no with Vaseline on it. The truth is, they don't want to think it over. If you are looking at a new car and a salesperson asks, "Anything I can help you with?" What do you say? "No, I am just looking." Or, "I am just thinking about it." No, you're not. All you're doing is waiting for the salesperson to leave so you can exit the car lot. It's human nature. I know we will encounter it in our meetings, which is why I press for an answer up front. I say, "Let me present my findings to you in a preliminary plan. Let's schedule the second meeting, and I will have a plan ready for you to review."

As mentioned, it takes time to draft a retirement plan, so usually I charge a fee to get started. Other times I do not, but that only happens under certain circumstances. The reason for the initial cost is because I believe payment for work is only fair. Second, it is a way to evaluate if the prospect is seriously interested. He may stay for a dozen meetings and seminars, but as soon as I present him with a fee, off he goes. Frankly, we do not like to do work for free. Who does? It's true, if you want to buy something from a commissioned salesperson, he will parachute into your yard to make sure you make the purchase. However, as soon as there is a problem, can you get that salesperson back to fix it? Of course not. Everyone knows this. It's warranty work. Nobody likes to do warranty work because they have already been paid for it.

We, on the other hand, do warranty work. We will not chase a prospect down the street, and we certainly will not parachute into his yard, and we will not spend twenty meetings trying to convince him to become a client. But once a prospect becomes a client, we work hard. We work as hard as anybody, and I am confident when I say it. Of course, that could be a story. After all, most prospects do not know us from Adam. But that is the way I do business. Prospects need to trust us. We require an up-front fee because we are going to invest our time and muscle ensuring a client's retirement is successful. If the prospect is a good fit, he will understand.

Some clients pretend to understand, or do understand our philosophy in theory, but when we meet for the second time, and the plan we present does not respond to their expectations, then there is trouble. We have touched on this before, and I will share a story about another couple we had as clients recently that helps to illustrate the point further.

We had a couple who was trying to compensate for having too much fun during their career years. They were still working when we met but hoped to retire in a year's time. Considering how much money they were earning, they had very little saved. So, we explained that to them; we set up a portfolio that had assets in equities, stocks, mutual funds; we transferred money from their 401(k). Mostly, we presented them with a plan that provided income for life and very little risk everywhere else. They could not afford risk, because they did not have the money saved for it.

A year passes. They retire. The market did not do very well that year, down 5 percent, and the money they had there did not deliver huge returns. They believed they should be making money all the time on the market. I told them no, the money invested in the market is designed to stay for the long term so it can ride the ups and downs. They said they could get 3 percent. I asked where.

They suggested our plan was unfit, that they did not make money that year. And it was true; they had not, because the assets in the money market were designed to deliver over a ten- to fifteen-year period, not a year. Over a longer course of time is when you bring in 6 to 7 percent returns.

I ask clients, "Do you want a plan that might work or a plan that will work?" Everyone always answers, naturally, that they want a plan that will work. I say, "Great, we have plans that will work. Because it is all math with me. The math has to work, and the plan must be provable."

PAPERWORK

Everyone, whether they are already retired, entering retirement, or still in their career years, should maintain a master list of crucial financial documents that contain information on mortgages, car loans, assets, properties, liabilities, and so on. At WSG, we provide a Generational Vault. This vault is online, in the cloud, and our clients can upload and download any document they wish. If you are not yet one of our clients, I always recommend keeping your documents in a safety deposit box. The fact is, death is chaotic. It is most helpful to your family to have your financial documents in one place, and for designated people to have access to them.

Furthermore, it's critical to review beneficiaries. Many people brush back against that recommendation, but we have found, time and again, that beneficiary policies are routinely out of date. For instance, there was a husband and wife in New York, both schoolteachers. They married in their forties. She had never married before, and neither had he. She had a sister and mother, but her father had passed away. She had made her mother and sister beneficiaries. Her mother died subsequently, and the policy stated that whoever was the surviving member of the two should receive the assets in the event of her own death. The wife assumed her beneficiary was her husband, but she was wrong. She had never updated her information. Later that year, she passed away suddenly. The court reviewed her policy and determined that the sister was the beneficiary, not the husband. The husband petitioned, claiming that was not what his wife wanted, that he was supposed to be the beneficiary. But all the court could do was review the policy, which confirmed the sister received all the assets. The husband did not get anything.

As easy as it is to procrastinate, do not. The task may seem daunting, and many people fear thorny or contentious issues with loved ones, but neglecting to organize your paperwork and keep it current can carry an unfortunate penalty.

In summary, it is best to begin with the end in mind and then work backward. You must have a plan in place before choosing investments. And you need a firm grasp of your resources and what you realistically can do with them. In short, you must organize your priorities and paperwork, and do so without delay.

Talk to your advisor. Put everything on the table—goals, expectations, and fears. Then devise a retirement plan. If we do the plan, we want to see documents, because then we know what we are working with; we know what we can do safely.

CHAPTER 3

NEW OPPORTUNITIES

ASK ANYONE BORN IN THE EARLY TO MID-TWENTIETH century how they planned to draw an income when they retired, and undoubtedly, they would answer with pensions, Social Security, and savings. These three elements, the three-legged stool of retirement, worked for generations of American workers. But the traditional model of retirement today is in sad shape, especially because pensions are becoming more and more rare, and the future of Social Security is questionable. Just in the last few months, many of the planning opportunities with

Social Security have fallen by the wayside as our country tries to decrease or even eliminate programs for the retired.

This chapter looks at different directions retirees can take in planning for the future, if they seize new opportunities to use their money wisely. The three-legged stool that once solidly supported retirement is growing increasingly wobbly; we are in a new era of financial planning. The search for new opportunities is critical.

But to understand what lies ahead, we must study that which is left behind. The three-legged stool of retirement is not simply a way to describe the means to an end. It encapsulates a full logic, a way of comprehending how things work, and then planning accordingly. The challenge, today, is to see that the old way of financial planning, and the logic that once held true for so many people, no longer applies. Of course, saving, earning, and taking advantage of opportunities are foundational and always will be. But what worked for the Bob Hope generation will not necessarily work for us.

Those who retired in the 1970s, even into the 1980s, had it made. All of them had a pension, most of them only worked for one or two companies, and they all could count on Social Security. Then, Social Security was a much larger part of income than it is today. And of course, most people had saved some money, but most of them did not plan to live thirty or more years while retired. Back then, in most cases, men could count on living seven, maybe eight years after retirement; women lived ten to twelve. That was it. Most retired people of that generation did not do the things we see retired people doing today. Retirement meant kicking back, relaxing, a lot of looking at one another. Hell, maybe that's why people did not live so long back then. I heard an old joke: Why do men die before women? Because they want to. I chuckle at that one because, in some cases, it is true. Of course, you can flip that joke on its head, and the men are the ones who are at the butt of it. At any rate, retirement a generation or two ago was a horse of a different color. People retired, got their affairs in order, and then, soon enough, they died. One thing people seldom had to worry about was ever running out of money. That was a result of the benefits programs they enjoyed and, frankly, the fact that most people just did not do that much and, in turn, did not spend that much in retirement. They didn't take ten cruises a year. They didn't buy second homes, cars, and new wardrobes. Today, however, we do. Remember, yesterday's luxuries are today's necessities.

It is only in the last fifteen to twenty years that we have seen sweeping changes in the way people spend their retirement. Today, it is practically a cottage industry. Couple that with the fact that we are living longer and just feel better and are more active—sixty is the new forty, and all that—and it is plain to see how dramatically the paradigm is shifting.

Today, the three-legged stool is a two-and-a-half-legged stool, and in some cases, a two-legged stool. Most people can no longer count on a defined benefits type of pension. That leaves Social Security, which everyone knows is uncertain, and the money people have saved. Today, the real retirement vehicles are 401(k)s, which, truly, are nothing more than IRAs. With 401(k)s, the employee decides how much money to set aside. Some employers try to sweeten the pot a little by saying that they will invest fifty cents for every dollar the employee sets aside. Other times, employers offer to match, dollar for dollar. There are dozens of scenarios. It comes down to this: "If you invest in your 401(k) with us, we will help you. If you do not, we will give you nothing." Stark terms. In essence, this allows the employers to move out from under the responsibility and cost structure of providing a pension plan. Actuaries drove the old defined benefit pension plans. Money had to be there, and actuaries had to make safe investments. Now, because employees control the cash, they can invest it in anything they want, and taking on much more risk becomes the norm. And this new system is good for employers, because it is far less expensive to offer 401(k)s than it is to provide company-wide pensions.

The shift away from pensions to 401(k)s broke the three-legged stool. Of the people I see today, whether they are in retirement or about to enter it, less than 15 to 20 percent have a defined benefits pension plan. That, coupled with the Social

Security shortfall that is current today, makes it crystal clear why the onus falls on savings, and whatever you managed to contribute already to your retirement plan.

Retirement plans differ. There are the IRAs and 401(k)s sponsored by employers; there are 403(b)s for teachers, doctors, nurses, and other folks who work for nonprofits; and there are 457 plans for municipal employees. We tend to favor IRAs because they offer an array of investment opportunities, whereas in employer-sponsored 401(k)s, for example, the employee is only able to utilize the investment choices available in their 401(k). The 401(k)s also tend to have hidden fees that can total as much as 3 to 4 percent, so it's important to look out for those.

Essentially, it boils down to each and every one of us having to make up more, and more, and more. We have to rely on our savings and 401(k)s because, most often, it is all we have. Now, when I say that Social Security has changed—that it is in trouble—everyone knows that. It's not an epiphany. For anyone under forty, it's a fact. In my opinion, people will always receive Social Security, but it is strained. Who knows, but maybe the start age will change to seventy-five. For the people I work with, retirees and soon-to-be retirees, there is positive news: I don't foresee much change in how and when Social Security will be paid in the near future. That said, retirees are being hit in other ways today. One of the biggest costs is medical care. We will discuss that in more detail soon.

Everything you might want to know about Social Security, and why it is in trouble today, traces back to Ida May Fuller. Fuller, a schoolteacher in Vermont, was the very first person to sign up for and receive Social Security. Her first check was for $22.54 in 1940. At that time, the average life expectancy for women was sixty-seven. For men, it was sixty-four. This means that the overall life expectancy for men and women was lower than the full retirement age for Social Security.

When Congress put together the Social Security bill, they looked at the average age of the retirement population versus the mean life expectancy. When Congress passed the law, the math made sense because, based on average life expectancy, they would not need to pay Social Security to individuals for an extended time. Well, Ida May Fuller went on to live until she was one hundred years old. She was an exception to the rule, of course. But one of the reasons we have trouble with Social Security today is because we have more people living longer in retirement, which strains the fund year after year. The good news for young people today is they will live a lot longer than most people did in 1940. The bad news is that Social Security might be harder to collect.

Again, for most people I deal with, the fifty-five and older set, Social Security is not in jeopardy. But for subsequent generations, it may be. It goes without saying that taxes will always be involved, regardless of your age—we need ever-increasing taxes just to provide the benefit. Everyone knows Social Security is a pay-as-you-go plan, that there is no Social Security pool of money. When I pay into Social Security, that money goes out to someone else. However, as people live longer in retirement, and hence increase the demands put on Social Security, the process will harden; the yield grows smaller than in the past. Some politicians even talk about means testing, which essentially means if you are lucky enough to have various sources of income, you might not be eligible for Social Security, so as to lighten the strain. That is a contentious issue. It angers people—as it should. If I pay Social Security all my working life under the agreement that I can depend on receiving my share when I am in retirement, and then when I am, my share is not available—well, that's a raw deal.

Collecting Social Security can be approached in a couple of different ways. Most everybody we deal with today was born between 1943 and 1954, generally speaking. The standard Social Security age to receive full benefits is sixty-six. The amount paid goes up and comes down depending on how old you are. For example, someone born in 1955 is eligible for full Social Security benefits at age sixty-six and two months. Conversely, if he wants to start receiving his benefits at sixty-two, he will receive less, roughly 75 percent of what he would at age sixty-six. If he were to get $2,000 at sixty-six, he'd only get $1,500 at sixty-two. In some cases, this approach makes sense, because it means he receives his benefit for a longer period, only at a reduced amount.

On the other hand, he can postpone his distribution until after he is sixty-six. Every year that he postpones, he receives an 8 percent increase. Now, with 8 percent interest per year, at age seventy, he is looking at receiving 32 percent more in benefits. That $2,000 is now $2,640. Keep in mind, though, that almost every year cost-of-living increases apply, so we have to plan for that, which we do—usually 3 to 4 percent. It is also important to remember that if he postpones collecting, he must supplement income from another source.

Many questions need answers when it comes to Social Security. However, this is not a Social Security book. The actual challenge is to calculate a breakeven point—the point at which it makes sense to collect for maximum benefits for the longest period. One thing a planning firm should help a client decide is whether it makes sense to take the benefits early, on time, or late. If you knew you were going to live to one hundred, it would make sense to wait until age seventy to collect.

Unfortunately, we don't know that. If we did, heck, it'd make our jobs a lot easier. My opinion is that it's best to wait as long as possible to collect. There are various reasons for that, but again, this is not a book on Social Security. The message is: talk to your advisor. If your advisor cannot provide counsel for Social Security, get a new advisor.

So, now that we know that pensions, by and large, are a relic of the past and that Social Security can provide only a weak safety net, it is time to consider personal savings and investments. From an advisor's standpoint, savings and investments are where we spend the most time. They require discipline and planning. If it were easy, everyone would be wealthy!

As I mentioned earlier in this book, if you spent your entire working life not saving, there is nothing I or any other advisor can do. I can only work with the assets available. Nevertheless, it happens all the time. People visit and tell me they have $300,000 and want to extract $30,000 per year, which over thirty years is 10 percent of all the money from their portfolio. Once I pick myself up off the ground and quit laughing, I say they have one chance: get lucky and die early.

I've been in this business for more than thirty years. Not once has someone come in to see me and said, "Bob, I have two goals. The first is to die, and the second is to die quickly." If someone said this, they would not need me; they'd need a shrink. Naturally, I use this analogy only to drive home my point, which is this: nobody wants to die early, but some financial plans do not coincide with living a long life. Drawing $30,000 from $300,000 for thirty years is just unrealistic.

"Do you want a plan that might work or a plan that will work?" I ask. And I get the same answer every time.

People want happy endings, and they want to hear good news. It's human nature. But in retirement, accepting reality is imperative. Most often, accepting reality—as hard as it can be—does indeed lead to happy endings. It's just a matter of execution.

Let me share a story that illustrates this point.

In 2006, a husband and wife named Joyce and Sam came to see me. Joyce said, "I have some money I want you to use in either investments or annuities. I don't care."

"Okay," I said.

"I've been working with a guy at a big Wall Street firm. I love him to death, so you cannot touch my mutual funds. They are to remain with him. Is that a deal?"

"Sure," I said. "I can do that."

The meeting continued, and she asked about returns.

"If you were to work with the equity part of my portfolio, what kind of returns do you think you could get on stocks and bonds?"

"I don't know," I said. "Probably 7 percent net after fees."

"My other guy told me he can get 10 percent."

"Well," I said, "you need to stay with him. Then you can sue him in ten years."

Despite the mild tension, the meeting continued. Joyce and Sam were the competitive types. I was looking through their account statement from her mutual-fund's guy because we were transferring some funds from that account to their initial income shortage.

I said, "Joyce, there is a line item here. I don't know what it is."

"I don't either," she said. "He's not charging me a fee." She did not know it, but her guy had charged an asset management fee on a mutual fund that he had been paid a commission on from the original purchase.

"Let's call him," I said. So we did. We dialed the 1-800 number and went through the preliminary queues and transfers for what seemed like nine years, and then finally we got a young guy on the horn, and I asked, "Hey, what is this? What does this acronym stand for?"

It was obvious he'd been asked the question before.

"That's a 2 percent financial planning fee. But Joyce and Sam agreed to it. They said it was okay."

Sam looked at me. "I do not have anything that shows that."

Too many times, because some financial firms slide so many papers over to you to sign, it is easy to overlook a crucial piece of information. In Joyce and Sam's case, they'd already paid commissions, and then the firm double-dipped and took out an account fee. What's more, a 2 percent advisor fee is enormous. Most advisors run at 1 percent, or maybe one and a quarter. So, 2 percent on top of commissions is offensive.

"You move every penny out of that account," Joyce said. "Immediately."

That was in 2006. Joyce and Sam have been clients ever since. They are my clients because the guy Joyce once claimed she loved to death was lying to her. First, his promise of 10 percent returns was unrealistic. Joyce did not know that, because she did not have returns with which to compare it. Nevertheless, the numbers were exaggerated and the math was bad. Second, he was not completely honest in charging her extra fees. These two mistakes can be disastrous. Math and honesty are paramount. Remember that.

I get clients because I tell the truth. I do not tell them a good story with a happy ending that has no roots in reality. I don't create a false image. People prefer to hear that everything is all right. If it is not all right, telling them that just makes matters worse.

When I sit down with a potential client, I tell them that despite the volatility of the market, despite the high taxes and uncertainties associated with Social Security, despite no longer having a pension, there is good news. You do not need to make 8 to 10 percent returns to enjoy the rest of your life. Some of my clients enjoy a successful retirement on 3 to 4 percent returns. How? They avoid losses.

I have mentioned how difficult it is to recover from market losses—if you lose 50 percent, you have to make 100 percent to get back to where you started. But if you can avoid losses altogether, you do not have to recover. Simply by avoiding losses, minimizing taxes, and using our "Income Bliss" model, which positions assets to consume over sequential time periods, we can create a terrific retirement with little or no risk. That is the good news: you do not need to take risks. Most people, however, think you do. Some people even want to take risks. Those people subscribe to Gardner's First Law.

Gardner's First Law stipulates that roughly 30 percent of people would rather lose money taking an aggressive posture and then talk about the loss over drinks at the country club than grow their money steadily. It's a wrongheaded approach, but it's the truth of the matter. Investment behavior is hard to mitigate. I can hear them now, "Oh, man. I lost $200,000 in the market. I got killed on that one." It is almost as if there is a perverse pleasure in play, and the true motivation working behind it all is simply the opportunity to boast about losing a ton of money over cocktails.

Our investment process is slow and methodical. People who look for high returns typically sit down in my office and ask about fees and hot picks. I am not interested in talking about hot picks, but I am happy to discuss fees.

We hire a money manager for a flat fee of $500 (no matter how large the account is), and our fees on top of that are another

0.75 percent. Some people say, "Holy cow. You charge as much as the money manager?"

I always respond, "The money manager only manages money. I manage you. My job is harder."

The truth of the matter is that we come wired from the factory to do the wrong thing at the wrong time. What happens when the stock market goes down? People sell. When do people want to buy stock? As an example, if your local market was having a two-for-one sale on tomato soup, and you loved tomato soup, you would buy every can in stock. However, when stocks drop in price, which creates a buying opportunity, what do we do? We panic, freeze. It's counterintuitive when you think about it. What's more, when *Money Magazine* picks the top ten mutual funds, it means they are trading at a sky-high price.

As I said, investment behavior poses many challenges. Being methodical requires planning. In the short term, we are tactical. In the long term, we are passive, as the market is efficient over long periods of time. But most investment behavior does not recognize planning as a vital piece in the retirement puzzle, when in truth, planning is much more important than investing. Many people invest first and plan second. That's wrong. Of course, vast numbers of fantastic investments exist. But how can someone invest if he does not even have a plan as to why he needs the money?

We have already talked about how we divide assets into the three buckets of income, liquidity, and legacy, and we will talk in more detail about planning for the different phases of retirement in the chapters to come.

In closing, we now know that the three-legged stool of retirement is not working for new retirees. With pensions largely out of the picture and Social Security under considerable strain, the focus of retirement planning falls squarely on the shoulders of savings. More than ever, people are expected to be in charge of investing for their retirement, yet many have not saved and lack the skills and inclination for investing. Not everyone, of course, wants to deal with investing, and that is fine, so long as, like a good CEO, they delegate the task to an advisor who acts in their best interest.

The three-legged stool of retirement may be broken, but for those who proceed with wisdom and good counsel, all is far from lost. In this new era, with the emphasis on personal responsibility for retirement planning, there are opportunities to seize—and to lose. At the end of the day, it comes down to planning, honesty, and math. With these in place, a good advisor always has his client's back.

CHAPTER 4

WHO'S GOT YOUR BACK?

AT THIS POINT IN THE BOOK, WE HAVE COVERED enough ground to understand why retirement planning is vital. We understand that retirement as we know it today is vastly different from retirement in the twentieth century. This information allows us to realize the importance of setting priorities and goals for the rest of our lives. In Chapter 3, we discussed how the three-legged stool of retirement—pensions, Social Security, and savings—is no longer sturdy, and that to enjoy this new phase in life, retirees must seize new opportunities and avoid undue losses.

In this chapter, we are going to examine why it is crucial that new retirees, as well as existing retirees already working with financial planners, explore their options when it comes to professional financial guidance. Retirement planning has no shortage of so-called experts spouting can't-lose prophecies, but the truth is, more than anything else, retirement requires a safe and methodical approach designed to provide income for life. We will highlight the perils of poor advice, whether it leads to investing recklessly or fearfully, and underscore why teamwork is essential in designing a solid financial plan for retirement.

To begin, I want to tell you a personal story that illustrates why second opinions are necessary. I always encourage my clients to seek second opinions. Why? Because it reinforces the quality of the work we do. Plenty of financial planners promise higher returns than we do, but they cannot back up those promises. We do not shoot for the moon, simply because, first, we know it is unnecessary to pull in high returns to live a happy retirement, and second, because our philosophy is to grow money slowly and safely. More than thirty years of experience demonstrates that our philosophy is the right philosophy; as a matter of fact, it is the only prudent way. When a client does seek a second opinion and comes back asking why such and such a firm can deliver higher returns than we can, I usually say it's because they live in a place called unreality. But frankly, at this point, if excessive numbers still persuade the client, it is probably better for her to go with the other guy. After all, I've laid out my plan and my philosophy at this stage. If the client does not think it is the proper plan for her, that is fine with me. At the end of the day, it comes down to math. If I show a client how I can deliver 6 percent returns over the long term while still producing income, and she wants 10 percent returns sooner because that's what another firm promised her, I can do the math for her. I can show her why our plan is provable and predictable, and why the other plan is not.

So, second opinions are essential. I learned that in 1985 when I was thirty-two years old. I went to the doctor for an insurance exam. The doctor had his stethoscope against my chest listening, it seemed like a lifetime. I'd heard since I was a kid about my heart murmur, but I grew up in rural South Carolina, a place where, unless you lost an arm to a farming or automobile accident, you did not go to the doctor. So I did not pay the murmur business too much mind. But in 1985, I had a family, and when the doctor told me I had a leaking heart valve, well, it scared the hell out of me.

He sent me to a cardiologist, who said I had a leaking aortic valve. He said it was okay for the time being, but it required monitoring. Eventually, it would need to be replaced.

I asked him what, exactly, that meant.

He told me if I were a bit older, they would replace my valve with a porcine valve, a pig valve. "But they don't last forever, that's the downside," he said. "But the good news is you would not need to take blood thinners."

Great, I thought. But what about now, when I am thirty-two?

"We typically use a synthetic valve. Merely because they last. Pretty much a lifetime guarantee."

But is that lifetime guarantee fifty years or thirty days? Who knows? I thought.

Lo and behold, eight years later, at age forty, I needed open heart surgery. I wasn't getting enough oxygen to my heart. I would eventually die of congestive heart failure if they did not operate. They gave me a St. Jude's valve, which saved my life. I've had it ever since. I do have to take blood thinners, but that is okay with me. However, a friend of mine in Denver, Doug, had the same diagnosis. His doctors told him pretty much what my doctors said. "It's the pig valve or the plastic valve."

Well, Doug was not satisfied with those options. He had learned about a Canadian technique using the natural aortic tissue to reconstruct the aortic valve, which prevented open-heart surgery. Essentially, they got to the aortic valve and did a bit of rewiring. Doug went to Canada and spoke with a cardiologist. In the end, the cardiologist came to Denver as a guest surgeon and completed the procedure successfully. Doug, of course, is fully recovered and does not need to take blood thinners every day.

This story dramatically illustrates the importance of soliciting second opinions. Doug's case could have turned out otherwise. He was fortunate. But either way, it is so critical to know what your options are and to make an informed decision based on facts. Outside of the emergency room, it is not quite as much a matter of life and death. But the importance remains. We are, after all, talking about the money that fuels the final stages of life. I tell people all the time that the worst thing that can happen when you get a second opinion is you'll feel better about the plan you have. We can feel good about our choices when we understand the facts and circumstances; it's just a matter of information. Unfortunately, in this day and age, men and women and young and old alike tend to spend more time planning their next vacation than they do their retirement.

And because many people do not spend time planning for retirement, when the time comes, they look for a quick fix, an easy answer. That leads to the preponderance of bad advice. In our culture, poor financial advice abounds. Remember, stupidity that's well packaged sounds profound.

Stockbrokers are now called financial planners. Why? Because the term "stockbroker" has negative connotations. Regardless of what you call them, these guys, the wire-house guys, are stockbrokers. They make transactions. Some make commissions; others do fee work. But most of them are trying to shoot the moon because they know they can trade for commissions, or they can make more money on fees.

Because stockbrokers earn based on the size of the accounts they hold, it makes sense for them to try to double the size of their accounts. Say, for example, they have a million-dollar account. If they make 1 percent, that's $10,000 per year. Why not double that account to $2 million? That increases the stockbroker's earning to $20,000. The client is happy; the stockbroker is happy.

But what happens if that $1 million turns into half a million dollars? What happens if you're a retiree dependent on that $1 million? Taking on a risk of this kind is counterproductive, especially if the goal is to provide income for life. Stockbrokers do not care about your income. They care about increasing the size of their accounts to bring more money in for themselves. Following the stockbrokers' investment strategy with their promise of 10 percent earnings, the best way for someone to quickly earn a million dollars from their portfolio is to start with an investment of $10 million—something most people can't afford.

Don't get me wrong; I am not suggesting that none of your money should be in the markets. But the money you do invest should not be touched for fifteen to twenty years. If it stays invested for a long time, even relatively small amounts that are less than $1 million can compound and earn a million dollars over time.

I give stockbrokers a hard time because they give bad advice. I know the difference between good advice and bad advice now, after thirty years in business. It's kind of like Edison inventing the light bulb. He failed time and again, over and over. But each time he failed, he was that much closer to success, to knowing what worked. A long career has allowed me to grow, make mistakes, and learn from them. Now I know the best advice is to make money slowly and methodically, to avoid risk and losses. I tell people that up front. I tell them, "Look, we do not need to hit home runs. We are not going to grow your wealth fast, because that usually does not work over the long haul. It might work, but then again, it might not." I ask, "Do you want a plan that will work or a plan that might work?"

"But I have conservative stocks," they respond incredulously.

"Jumbo shrimp," I say. "There's no such thing as conservative stocks. It's an oxymoron."

Typically, when someone says he has conservative stocks, he is talking about staid companies that have been around for more than one hundred years. You think of the Dow Jones industrials rather than Nasdaq. These types of stocks pay a dividend, and you can rationalize a little loss in value because the dividend offsets it. A tech stock, on the other hand, is intellectual property; there is no brick-and-mortar attached to the company, and there is nothing to offset losses.

Dividend companies, the Dow Jones industrials, are huge companies that have been operating for a long time. Procter *&* Gamble is an example. If a big company like Procter *&* Gamble provides reliable dividends, it is considered a conservative stock to own. But, in 2008, when the S&P 500 was down 38 percent, the Dow Jones was down 34 percent. Sure, those stocks still had their dividends, but the price of the stock was slashed by a third. Some stocks are less risky than others, but there is no such thing as a conservative stock.

Remember, if you lose 40 percent in the markets, you need to make 67 percent to get back to where you started. The goal is to identify less risky stocks and bonds, hold on to them for the long haul, and let the market play for time.

When people do have their money in the market, and they start using up their dividends, we call them "asset huggers." Let's say I have a client with $300,000 in dividend stocks that he is using for income. I ask him what his dividend rate is.

"Three percent," he says. "I get $9,000 per year to supplement my income, and I want to stay this way because I have total liquidity in this account. But you want to put me in an annuity? And on top of that, you have fees? Here, I have complete liquidity."

"Listen, Mr. Asset Hugger," I say. "You don't have any liquidity."

"How's that?"

"Because you are using that $9,000 for income. As soon as you cash that out, you have zero income. Where will you get income from next? You need to use another asset."

We call these people asset huggers because they are hugging the asset to get their income. Now, each client is of course entitled to his opinion, and we respect that opinion. But income without liquidity does not fit into the "Income Bliss" model. We design portfolios from conservative to aggressive, and we do it based on when money is needed and how it will be spent.

Say, for example, you are my client and sixty-five years old. I have you set up in a small mutual fund portfolio that we will use twenty-five years from now when you are ninety. Age has nothing to do with it. When you need the money has everything to do with it. If you don't need the money for twenty-five years, I can manage the fund like I would manage the fund for a forty-year-old. A forty-year-old has a twenty-five, thirty-year horizon. Markets are efficient over time. We can go through the ups and downs, the fluctuations. We can manage the money passively because we know we are going to be successful over an extended period. We can be tactical, meaning that if we sense danger, we can get out. It is important to remember that I am trying to avoid losses. I will sacrifice gains to avoid losses. Over an extended period, if the money will be used in the last phase of a person's life, most likely it will be in a passive portfolio that lets the markets do the work.

Everything is time with us. We have a certain amount of time to work. We use a segment strategy that breaks the money into income, liquidity, and legacy. Income pays your day-to-day expenses.[2] Liquidity covers emergencies, special wants and needs, and unforeseen expenses. Anything that's left goes toward your legacy—what you want to leave behind. Once we have this organized, we know what is provable; we know what is accessible and when.

Bad advice comes in many forms, from insurance salespeople to bankers. Neither provides the type of comprehensive solutions found at a fiduciary firm. Insurance salesmen don't have the credentials to extol financial advice with sound virtue. They need to sell insurance to earn an income, so that is what they do, whether or not it is what's best for the client. Banks are a beautiful place to put money until you decide where it really needs to go.

Firms measure investments in two different ways. The first is through suitability, which means the value of an investment is based on the firm's evaluation of it. If you work with a Merrill Lynch rep and he sells you a suitable investment, that investment is suitable to Merrill Lynch and, theoretically, you. But you, as the client, do not come first. A rep is paid a commission on stocks and mutual funds. When his company evaluates and signs off on stocks and mutual funds, they are deemed suitable. You can see why a client's best interest may be compromised.

---

2   Income Bliss Model, wealth2k.com.

The second measure is fiduciary. This means the firm must prove to an arbitration court that an investment recommendation is sound for the client first and foremost. There are no ulterior motives or associated commissions.

It goes without saying that a financial advisor at a fiduciary firm might be a terrible advisor. Alternatively, a representative at a suitability firm who is working on commissions might be the most knowledgeable advisor known to man. It's a toss-up.

The one thing that grounds us as a fiduciary firm is that our planning is designed to deliver income for the life of our clients. If we do that and our clients are pleased with their returns, we fulfill our fiduciary duty. It's a simple approach to a complex problem. We account for your money properly, so we do not need to be the greatest advisors, because we are dealing with math and predictability.

Take all of these sources of bad advice and add to the mix the media and the internet—it is easy to see how people are caught up in bad advice. The media is always looking for hot takes and one-size-fits-all solutions, and the internet is just so much noise—information overload from dubious sources. All advisors are not created equal, and from a client's perspective, it's hard to know whom to trust. For many clients, it comes down to who the players are and how much compensation they receive.

The players are compensated either by commissions or fees or both. One is not necessarily better than the other, but it is important to understand with whom you are working. My opinion is that commissions are endemic to the industry. If you are a commissions-based rep, once you receive your commission, it is done, and on to the next one you go. You start over and sell another product and get a new commission. That is where manipulation comes into play. If the commissions rep is looking at his earnings first and the client's second, he may ask you to buy a mutual fund, for example, that provides him with a new commission but does little good for you. The value of the mutual fund is secondary. The sale is what's paramount. Of course, that is a pessimistic scenario. There are times when the commission rep's recommendation is legitimate and you should buy. It is just difficult always to see clearly the motivations behind the transaction.

I use this as a cautionary tale often in my seminars. I hold up an invitation circulated by one of my competitors. The invitation has on it the company that sponsors my competitor's dinner seminars.

I ask the audience, "Have all of you received this yet? If not, you most likely will, or one like it. Think about it, folks. If you have a business sponsoring, and that means paying cash, to put on a seminar and pay for dinner, when you go into this person's office, whose product do you think they are going to recommend?"

That competitor is not a financial planner—but a salesperson. If a company invests money in a dinner seminar, rest assured they expect something in return. Even an honest advisor will work this way when he has a client in his office following a sponsored seminar. The advisor may understand that placing the client at a certain firm is best, but because the sponsoring firm got the client in the room, the advisor is somewhat beholden to that firm. There is a limitation to do what can be done and also a particular bias. That's just human nature, I suppose. Everyone is biased. You, me, even the most objective person is still subjective. But if you get back to math, and you consider the ratings of the firms with which you conduct business, it does not matter that there is subjectivity sometimes as long as the numbers are the main focus.

We don't accept sponsorships from companies. Our only method of income with respect to investment portfolios is through fees—when you win, we win. We are an RIA (registered investment advisor) firm, which means we do have fees, and we do disclose them. Does that mean we are smarter than the next firm? No. Does it mean we're better than the next firm? No. We just believe that this model benefits our clients by closely aligning our goals with respect to their portfolio management. Full stop.

But we are not fee-only; we are fee-based. The fee-only advisor cannot manage insurance affairs. He cannot do comprehensive estate planning. We are fee-based, but we're also a hybrid firm. All our investments are on a fee basis. Annuities, insurance, long-term care—these we do on a commission basis. It's almost like a finder's fee. Or, to use a dated analogy, it's what a travel agent did. Every dollar invested in insurance goes to work for the client. The insurance company compensates us, not the client.

We are a hybrid firm because we must utilize a whole universe of products to provide powerful, personal advice. If I don't have the ability, because I am a fee-based-only firm and thus do not have the appropriate licenses to place every product in a client's plan that needs to be there, then I cannot live up to the philosophy on which I have built my firm. The client cannot achieve his or her goals and needs. In other words, they can't maximize their financial potential.

A good advisor tailors a plan to the client's unique needs and objectives. He establishes rapport and trust and provides regular, consistent reviews. We care foremost about the best interests of the client, and the client maintains control and gains experience. When emotions run high, as they sometimes can, especially when lifestyle expectations change, and spouses shed tears and anger flares, a client requires a steady hand, a coach on whom he or she can rely. After all, every world-class athlete has a coach or mentor. I think of our role as advisors in a similar way.

We coach our clients on the decisions they need to make to have income for life. We delegate responsibility among our team members. We have a director of marketing who handles client events, referrals, seminars, and classes. The director of marketing is typically the first person to have contact with a prospective client, and so it's essential to the firm. We have a customer-service manager who maintains our clients' information and keeps clients in touch and informed. And we have a director of operations who keeps a record of our clients' portfolios and statements. Every time a client visits, we have an updated report to present. All of this effort ensures that our clients receive the very best advice and the most dedicated service. We have a team; that's the important thing. Our team takes care of everything from the time a client comes in to see us—no matter if it is from a seminar or as a referral—for the next twenty to forty years.

We do the best we can, every day. We love what we do and we care about our clients. That's what it is all about. It's what will keep us motivated and passionate about providing superior financial advice, for now and for years to come.

MOST PEOPLE DO NOT WANT TO PAY HIGH FEES. Who can blame them? But fees are part of doing business with a financial advisor. Granted, some advisors charge too much, especially those who do little to manage a client's portfolio actively. Other advisors pull the wool over their clients' eyes by claiming they do not charge fees, only to bury the charges in a sea of paperwork while calling the fee by another name. I have had clients visit me and say that their rep from one of the big firms does not charge a fee.

"Really?" I say. "Let me show you here, on page 12 or 107, hidden here in the prospectus. You're paying 2 percent. It's just under the hood. What's more, it is a real drag on performance."

Most people don't know this and understandably feel duped. We are up front about our fees, why we charge what we do, and what a client can expect in exchange.

The bottom line—advice is not free. If a firm truly does not charge fees and they do not bury costs in their prospectus under a different name, then that firm is not going to be in business very long.

We have already reviewed why typical investor behavior can be such a scourge on effective retirement planning.

Even so, most people, sometimes against their better judgment, just cannot move away from risky investments that promise high returns. It is our job to deliver a plan that circumvents that mentality, to illustrate why high returns are temporary and elusive and that retirement planning is for the long haul. It sounds reasonable, but many times we must steer clients clear of ruin. That's why we charge a 0.75 percent fee. We actively manage portfolios; we look at them every day. We are time-tactical, looking for better options and safe investments.

Regardless, people who come to us are sometimes unable to digest the fact that we charge fees. Of course, when they come from another firm, they've been paying fees all along, but they are just not used to seeing them called fees. In some cases, a client may have little commissions to pay, but other expenses are sucking away his return.

Alternatively, if a client finds a fund in which the expenses are buried, those expenses often total more than average fees, sometimes as high as 4 percent—it's only that the payments are broken up into various charges and buried under the hood.

Sometimes, a client wants to manage the money personally, without professional advice. They want the portfolio to remain passive and, in turn, remove fees from the equation. These funds, like the Vanguard s&p 500 fund, are fine if that is what you want to do. But you receive a lack of counsel with these funds, and they remain passive through good times and bad.

In late 1999, I had a client named Bill. We were managing a $1 million portfolio for him. He came in one day and said, "Bob, no offense, but I just don't think I need you."

I smiled.

"I am going to put my million dollars in a Vanguard s&p 500 fund."

At the time, the fees associated with the Vanguard fund were small, hovering near one-fifth of 1 percent—and they are even lower today.

Bill said, "You and the money manager you work with charge 2 percent fees; if I am in the Vanguard fund, I do not need to do as well to make money."

"True," I said. "But you are not going to have anyone guiding you. What about the money you will need out of your portfolio?"

"Well," he said, "I plan on taking $50,000 out a year, 5 percent of my portfolio. I don't need advice to do that. I think I am in good shape."

"Okay," I said. "Good luck."

Now, I don't know if Bill did this, but for the sake of the argument, let's assume he transferred $1 million to the s&p

500 mutual fund with Vanguard. Let's also say he withdrew his $50,000 in April every year. We know for a fact, because of the market's performance during those years, that without making any withdrawals, Bill's portfolio at the end of 2002 was worth $650,000 in round numbers.

That's accounting for none of the withdrawals Bill made. But he did make withdrawals, one in 2000, 2001, and 2002. If you subtract $150,000 from $650,000 you are left with $500,000.

However, his $50,000 withdrawal now comprises 10 percent of the remaining portfolio. It's not a question of if he will run out of money, because he will. It's a matter of when.

This story proves two points. First, being overly fee-conscious is not always the best way to manage a portfolio. Investors miss opportunities and accrue losses. The second point highlights the importance of remaining vigilant when it comes to your sequence of returns.

Simply put, the concept of sequence of returns notes that even if short-term volatility averages out into positive long-term returns, an investor can still be in trouble if the sequence of those returns is negative. In Bill's case, because his withdrawals occur every year, it is not enough for his returns to average out over time. His portfolio will be empty before the positive returns even arrive.

Initial Balance: $500,000.00
Withdrawal Rate: 0%

Year	Beginning Balance	Historical Return	Annual Withdrawal
1999	$500,000	19.53%	$ —
2000	$597,650	−10.14%	$ —
2001	$537,048	−13.03%	$ —
2002	$467,071	−23.34%	$ —
2003	$358,057	26.36%	$ —
2004	$452,440	8.99%	$ —
2005	$493,115	2.97%	$ —
2006	$507,760	13.62%	$ —
2007	$576,917	3.53%	$ —
2008	$597,282	−38.49%	$ —
2009	$367,388	23.48%	$ —
2010	$453,651	12.83%	$ —
2011	$511,855	0.00%	$ —
2012	$511,855	13.35%	$ —
2013	$580,187	29.59%	$ —
2014	$751,864	11.36%	$ —
2015	$837,276	−0.73%	$ —
2016	$831,164	9.54%	$ —
2017	$910,457	19.44%	$ —
Total	**$1,087,450**	**4.17%**	**$ —**

Initial Balance: $500,000.00
Withdrawal Rate: 5%

Year	Beginning Balance	Historical Return	Annual Withdrawal
1999	$500,000	19.53%	$25,000
2000	$572,650	−10.14%	$25,000
2001	$489,583	−13.03%	$25,000
2002	$400,791	−23.34%	$25,000
2003	$282,246	26.36%	$25,000
2004	$331,646	8.99%	$25,000
2005	$336,461	2.97%	$25,000
2006	$321,454	13.62%	$25,000
2007	$340,236	3.53%	$25,000
2008	$327,246	−38.49%	$25,000
2009	$176,289	23.48%	$25,000
2010	$192,682	12.83%	$25,000
2011	$192,403	0.00%	$25,000
2012	$167,403	13.35%	$25,000
2013	$164,751	29.59%	$25,000
2014	$188,501	11.36%	$25,000
2015	$184,915	−0.73%	$25,000
2016	$158,565	9.54%	$25,000
2017	$148,692	19.44%	$25,000
Total	**$152,598**		**$475,000**

Initial Balance: $500,000.00
Withdrawal Rate: 0%

Year	Beginning Balance	Historical Return	Annual Withdrawal
2002	$500,000	−23.34%	$—
2008	$383,300	−38.49%	$—
2011	$235,768	0.00%	$—
2007	$235,768	3.53%	$—
2009	$244,090	23.48%	$—
2001	$301,403	−13.03%	$—
2014	$262,130	11.36%	$—
1999	$291,908	19.53%	$—
2012	$348,918	13.35%	$—
2013	$395,498	29.59%	$—
2000	$512,526	−10.14%	$—
2017	$460,556	19.44%	$—
2004	$550,088	8.99%	$—
2006	$599,541	13.62%	$—
2005	$681,198	2.97%	$—
2016	$701,430	9.54%	$—
2010	$768,346	12.83%	$—
2003	$866,925	26.36%	$—
2015	$1,095,447	−0.73%	$—
Total	**$1,087,450**		**$—**

Initial Balance: $500,000.00
Withdrawal Rate: 5%

Year	Beginning Balance	Historical Return	Annual Withdrawal
2002	$500,000	−23.34%	$25,000
2008	$358,300	−38.49%	$25,000
2011	$195,390	0.00%	$25,000
2007	$170,390	3.53%	$25,000
2009	$151,405	23.48%	$25,000
2001	$161,955	−13.03%	$25,000
2014	$115,852	11.36%	$25,000
1999	$104,013	19.53%	$25,000
2012	$99,327	13.35%	$25,000
2013	$87,587	29.59%	$25,000
2000	$88,504	−10.14%	$25,000
2017	$54,530	19.44%	$25,000
2004	$40,130	8.99%	$25,000
2006	$18,738	13.62%	$25,000
2005	$(3,710)	2.97%	$25,000
2016	$(28,820)	9.54%	$25,000
2010	$(56,570)	12.83%	$25,000
2003	$(88,827)	26.36%	$25,000
2015	$(137,242)	−0.73%	$25,000
Total	**$(161,240)**		**$475,000**

Initial Balance: $500,000.00
Withdrawal Rate: 0%

Year	Beginning Balance	Historical Return	Annual Withdrawal
2011	$500,000	0.00%	$—
2013	$500,000	29.59%	$—
2003	$647,950	26.36%	$—
2012	$818,750	13.35%	$—
2001	$928,053	−13.03%	$—
1999	$807,127	19.53%	$—
2002	$964,759	−23.34%	$—
2017	$739,585	19.44%	$—
2004	$883,360	8.99%	$—
2009	$962,774	23.48%	$—
2007	$1,188,833	3.53%	$—
2015	$1,230,799	−0.73%	$—
2010	$1,221,814	12.83%	$—
2016	$1,378,573	9.54%	$—
2008	$1,510,089	−38.49%	$—
2006	$928,856	13.62%	$—
2000	$1,055,366	−10.14%	$—
2005	$948,352	2.97%	$—
2014	$976,518	11.36%	$—
Total	**$1,087,450**		**$—**

Initial Balance: $500,000.00
Withdrawal Rate: 5%

Year	Beginning Balance	Historical Return	Annual Withdrawal
2011	$500,000	0.00%	$25,000
2013	$475,000	29.59%	$25,000
2003	$590,553	26.36%	$25,000
2012	$721,222	13.35%	$25,000
2001	$792,505	−13.03%	$25,000
1999	$664,242	19.53%	$25,000
2002	$768,968	−23.34%	$25,000
2017	$564,491	19.44%	$25,000
2004	$649,228	8.99%	$25,000
2009	$682,594	23.48%	$25,000
2007	$817,867	3.53%	$25,000
2015	$821,737	−0.73%	$25,000
2010	$790,739	12.83%	$25,000
2016	$867,191	9.54%	$25,000
2008	$924,921	−38.49%	$25,000
2006	$543,919	13.62%	$25,000
2000	$593,000	−10.14%	$25,000
2005	$507,870	2.97%	$25,000
2014	$497,954	11.36%	$25,000
Total	**$529,521**		**$475,000**

Initial Balance: $500,000.00
Withdrawal Rate: 0%

Year	Beginning Balance	Historical Return	Annual Withdrawal
2013	$500,000	29.59%	$—
2003	$647,950	26.36%	$—
2002	$818,750	–23.34%	$—
2011	$627,653	0.00%	$—
2017	$627,653	19.44%	$—
2007	$749,669	3.53%	$—
2000	$776,133	–10.14%	$—
2008	$697,433	–38.49%	$—
2014	$428,991	11.36%	$—
2001	$477,724	–13.03%	$—
2010	$415,477	12.83%	$—
2016	$468,782	9.54%	$—
2015	$513,504	–0.73%	$—
2006	$509,756	13.62%	$—
1999	$579,184	19.53%	$—
2012	$692,299	13.35%	$—
2005	$784,721	2.97%	$—
2009	$808,027	23.48%	$—
2004	$997,752	8.99%	$—
Total	**$1,087,450**		**$—**

Initial Balance: $500,000.00
Withdrawal Rate: 5%

Year	Beginning Balance	Historical Return	Annual Withdrawal
2013	$500,000	29.59%	$25,000
2003	$622,950	26.36%	$25,000
2002	$762,160	−23.34%	$25,000
2011	$559,272	0.00%	$25,000
2017	$534,272	19.44%	$25,000
2007	$613,134	3.53%	$25,000
2000	$609,778	−10.14%	$25,000
2008	$522,946	−38.49%	$25,000
2014	$296,664	11.36%	$25,000
2001	$305,365	−13.03%	$25,000
2010	$240,576	12.83%	$25,000
2016	$246,442	9.54%	$25,000
2015	$244,953	−0.73%	$25,000
2006	$218,164	13.62%	$25,000
1999	$222,878	19.53%	$25,000
2012	$241,407	13.35%	$25,000
2005	$248,634	2.97%	$25,000
2009	$231,019	23.48%	$25,000
2004	$260,262	8.99%	$25,000
Total	**$258,660**		**$475,000**

Long story short, I don't want to work with people who are more concerned about fees than they are about the performance of their portfolios. I don't apologize for fees, because we more than earn them back. A good advisor pays for his fees or does even better. Costs included in a mutual fund, on the other hand, can be a drain on a portfolio's performance.

Mutual funds emerged in the 1920s. They provided the first opportunity for people to pool money into a diversified fund, to use diversification to their advantage. They were not popular initially. In fact, it was not until the 1960s that anybody began to use them.

The reason for that is because most people did not know what mutual funds were. Mutual funds were designed to allow people to purchase a basket of stocks. In fact, most mutual funds, up until thirty-odd years ago, were all stock funds. In the sixties, mutual funds were much cheaper than they are today, and they really did their job. People who were not quite knowledgeable about them, but nonetheless wanted to invest, had no problem paying companies large commissions for buying and selling stocks. A broker was paid to purchase a fund-stock, and he was paid to sell it. When he sold it, he bought another one. The whole enterprise existed, thanks to commissions, and was repeated over and over.

Today, mutual funds are expensive. They exist mostly to attract assets, which is why there are so many big mutual fund complexes like American Funds, T. Rowe Price, and Fidelity, who have three or four hundred mutual funds. People like to buy a certain size, in various geographical locations, so it becomes almost like having a bank on every corner. Having a family of mutual funds makes it easier for a client to add to his collection. But these funds are more expensive now, and they routinely underperform.

Another dark secret of the mutual fund industry is survivorship bias. Survivorship bias means that unsuccessful funds are terminated, mostly liquidated and moved into a different fund. They destroy the fund's history. When mutual fund complexes highlight their returns, they do not take into account survivorship bias, meaning they only tally the returns of the surviving funds. That is why there is always the caveat stating that past performance is not indicative of nor guarantees future results. The same holds true for all of us—fee advisors, commission-based consultants, everyone.

More to the point, however, is that the mutual fund industry has morphed into a money-making cartel. Complexes add fees to the overall costs of funds and conceal the fees within the umbrella of a prospectus, so investors do not see them. And overall, the performance has been weak over time. Some of that is due to investors making poor choices; they don't stay the course. Over the last twenty years, for example, the return of the S&P is a little less than 10 percent. But the return for the average investor is less than 4 percent. What does that mean? It means current mutual funds do not help the average investor. We hear that it is time to sell when the market is low and buy when it's high, which is backward. If a mutual fund comes in as the top mutual fund one year, you can all but guarantee that the next year it will fall to a lower position. But what do people do? They buy it. And when the market is down, people sell rather than buy more. This behavior is why we anticipate that a mutual fund in the top quartile of performance for a particular period of time will be in the bottom quartile of performance in the next five to ten years. It's been proven, time and again.

Remember, there are two main ways to manage equities and mutual funds: passively, which lets the markets work over long periods, and tactically, which is where you monitor the market actively; you move in and out as you see fit. We focus on active time-segmented management, buying stocks/funds within the client's chosen portfolio and only making changes as market volatility dictates.

CHAPTER 5

WEALTH THREATS

AT THIS POINT, I HOPE YOU UNDERSTAND THAT ONE of the most important elements of investing and managing money for the retirement phase of your life is learning how to handle and avoid risks. Risks are an inherent part of investing, and as we age, the risks associated with our health and lifestyle increase. So, when the retirement phase of life is upon us, it is vital to understand how to manage those risks while developing resources relegated to the income, liquidity, and legacy buckets of your portfolio.

This chapter will provide an overview of specific risks to the retiree's portfolio. The largest and most common risks include taxes, money management fees, and healthcare costs. Other risks exist, of course, and must be managed wisely, but more often than not, portfolios are severely hampered when taxes, fees, and healthcare costs are accounted for unscrupulously.

In 2007, a retired dentist named Louis attended one of my seminars. Louis had been very successful; he had two gorgeous homes and a $1.2 million portfolio. After the seminar, Louis and I spoke, and he told me he wanted to have a meeting. I said great, and he came to see me the next week. In our first meeting, Louis said he was taking $9,000 per month from his portfolio. That comes out to roughly $108,000 per year. I gave him my die-quickly line.

"Louis, unless you get lucky and die quickly, you're going to run out of money."

He looked at me for a minute, unsure what to say. He squinted his eyes like a fox and then exhaled. He knew he had a problem; he knew his portfolio would not support his lifestyle. The problem was, he did not know what to do. If he did not wish to change his lifestyle nor his expectations of what his retirement would look like, how could he make his money last? I repeated my die-quickly line, and this time, it hit home. Louis's eyes widened. He may have turned a little pale. Pale or not, the issue was obvious now. It stood there like an elephant stamping its feet in my office.

I've said that the goal of my first meeting with a potential client is to decide if we will have a second meeting. In the first meeting, I ask the client to explain how he is currently managing his money—where it is, with whom, how much. I also determine if the client's personality and philosophy line up with mine. In the second meeting, I demonstrate how I can help. I present a limited plan to the client.

In Louis's case, while he recognized he had a problem, he was not ready to make the appropriate changes. I said, "Louis, $108,000 is too much. We can probably get $75,000, and that is if I am more aggressive than I like to be."

"Bob," Louis said, "I cannot live on that."

"Well," I said, "you are going to run out of money. Now, don't shoot the messenger here. I am not telling you what you can or cannot live on. I want to help you, but I will not be a party to your failure." When it comes to setting meetings with new clients, we look for chemistry, realistic goals, sufficient worth, and our ability to add value. In Louis's case, his goals (income) were not consistent with his assets.

He had already made up his mind, anyway. We shook hands and parted. Fast-forward a couple of months. My wife is a realtor, and she and I were in Columbia, South Carolina, for a conference she was attending. I tagged along, intent on enjoying the weekend. It turns out, though, that Louis's wife was also a realtor and attending the same conference. One day, I am sitting in the hotel lobby, nursing an ice-cold IPA, when I hear, "Hey, Bob."

"Bob," the voice said again. "It's me, Louis."

I looked at Louis funny because after so much time had passed and meeting him like this, out of context, it took me a minute to remember who he was. But then he started saying, "I am going to call you. I want to work with you."

"That's fine," I said. We broke apart and went on to our rooms. My wife was excited. "You got a client, how great!"

"He's not coming in," I said. "He just didn't know what to say to me down there, so he said he wanted to work with me. It's easier that way, to say, 'I'm coming to see you,' instead of, 'Sorry we couldn't work together.' It's human nature."

Well, I've been wrong once before, and here I was wrong again. Three weeks later, I get a call from Louis. Now, keep in mind that when we first met, when Louis had a $1.2 million portfolio, it was before the stock market crash. And at the time when he called me, the market was still getting crushed. We talked for a minute and set up a meeting. Long story short, his $1.2 million was down to $750,000. Between withdrawals and just complete losses, Louis watched almost $400,000 disappear in a couple of months.

Despite the severe loss, my perspective on how to manage Louis's portfolio had not changed. I presented him with more or less the same plan I had before, only instead of $75,000 we were taking $50,000 per year. And that was pushing it to the limit.

Louis accepted, albeit with his tail between his legs. Ever since then, whenever we talk, he always says he wishes he had taken our advice the first time around.

Good money management, risk-averse money management that provides an income for life, does not allow for "shoot for the moon" investments. Some people need that kind of action to feel as if their advisors are managing their portfolios actively. We don't use that approach. That's not to say we're perfect; we're not. But when we manage your money by managing risks and win by avoiding losses, we can and do provide a model that delivers income for life. It's just that easy—and yet somehow, for many investors, still so hard.

Many of the "millionaires next door" lost much of their assets during the recession. Why? Because they were either too aggressive or had stayed in the market too long. Or, they took their money out too soon. Many were so shell-shocked that they sat on their nest egg and didn't act until they felt the security of everyone else acting—and of course by then, it was too late. Whichever way you look at it, many people listened to traditional advice, meaning they listened to the stockbroker, the Wall Street side of the house.

The Wall Street side of the house says that over long periods, equities return more than fixed investments. And it's true. Since 1927, the S&P has returned about 10 percent. But that's nearly one hundred years. In all my years of retirement investment planning, I've not had one client come to me and say, "I don't need any money for ninety years. This investing is great in theory, and people love to talk about the market's behavior, but it's not my approach."

Remember Gardner's First Law: people would rather lose money in the market and talk about it over drinks than make money slowly in a boring fashion, such as treasury bonds, CDs, money markets, and fixed annuities. Investor behavior, again, plays a large role in a portfolio's chance of success. Those behaviors, when coupled with attitudes in the media about investing, are the two chief hurdles to truly acquiring wealth.

After all, if you have saved money, Social Security, and, hopefully, a pension, you can afford to be a conservative investor in retirement. I always tell people, "You may not own any equities, but mutual funds are fine as long as the time frame is long enough to navigate multiple market cycles." That's the way we build portfolios using the "Income Bliss" model. That's what we do, exactly.

As mentioned, risk management is a crucial function of a financial advisor. So much is at stake as retirees face a variety of risks to their economic well-being. The story about Louis, the dentist, highlights market risk. And there are many other risks:

- Inflation risk
- Interest-rate risk

- Taxes
- Hidden investment fees
- Medical and long-term costs
- The likelihood of longevity—Retirees these days speak of their fear of living too long and outlasting their resources.

Let's unpack some of these risks.

INFLATION RISKS

Inflation risk is the simple fact that every day our purchasing power erodes. Currently, the inflation rate is extremely low, but inflation will rise, and inflation itself is here to stay. We forecast and plan for about 3 to 4 percent inflation per year. For example, imagine a client who has a portfolio providing $30,000 annually. At 4 percent inflation, in eighteen years, that client will need $60,000 to have the same purchasing power that $30,000 affords today. Most portfolios do not produce that kind of revenue jump.

Inflation is the silent killer of portfolios. It is insidious because it is slow, kind of like when you boil a frog. Toss a frog in boiling water and it will jump right out. If you put the frog in lukewarm water, however, and just increase the temperature incrementally over time, the frog will stay put and, eventually, boil. Of all the risks a portfolio faces, inflation can be the deadliest. It's like when I told my twenty-five-year-old daughter, who is diabetic, that unless she changed her habits, she had a good chance of being dead by the time she was forty-five. Forty-five is a long way from twenty-five, so it did not hit home—it did not truly scare her. Forty-five seems like a lifetime away, but it is not. Inflation risk is strenuous because, even though people know it is there, and that it harms their portfolios, they have a hard time worrying about it because it moves slowly, and its adverse effects feel far away. It is incumbent upon the advisor to talk to their clients about spendable dollars and what those dollars will buy.

Interest-rate risk means, essentially, the danger of going broke slowly. As inflation increases and our purchasing power diminishes, the only way to earn money is to bring in returns higher than what the inflation rate is at that time. So, for example, if the inflation rate is 3 percent, and you are bringing in 3 percent returns, you are breaking even. If the inflation rate is 3 percent, and you are bringing in 0.5 percent, well, you are going broke slowly. Planning for interest-rate risk means measuring inflation, taking the subsequent increase in interest rates into account, and allocating assets accordingly.

Bond risk correlates with interest-rate risk. We have been in a bond bull market for thirty years, but when interest rates go up, the value of a current bond will decrease. For example, if you have a $100,000 bond that produces 4 percent interest for

$4,000—when interest rates increase to 5 percent, the bond is worth less because it is possible to buy a $100,000 bond that produces $5,000. The owner of the 4 percent bond has to discount his bond to make it salable. Essentially, for every 1 percent increase in interest rates, the value of a bond drops by 10 percent. People come to me and say their money is in bonds, so there is no risk. But there is a risk. The challenge is to create a portfolio that grows a set amount, thereby keeping pace with inflation and alleviating interest-rate risks.

TAXES

Taxes pose a significant threat to a portfolio; they are a drain. And, most likely, we will see a tax increase in the future. Why would anyone defer taking money out of an IRA, which is taxable, if taxes are going to increase? That is why many people consider changing from a traditional IRA to a Roth. For example, let's say you have $100,000 in an IRA. If you take that $100,000 out, you take home $70,000 and pay $30,000 in taxes. The $70,000 you take out today will never be taxed again. Contrast that to the 40 percent you would potentially pay ten years from now. If we assume taxes are going up, why not take the money out today and put it elsewhere?

Regardless of where people sit politically and how they feel about paying taxes, most can agree that taxes hurt a portfolio.

But many people cannot pull the trigger; the thought of paying the tax man, be it for $30,000 or $40,000, makes them quiver and they'd rather postpone it, to kick the can a bit down the road. This approach is important to consider, however, because obviously, if we have options to create tax-free income for a client, the client is better off moving her money out of her IRA and into the tax-free investment. Know this: we strive to make as much income tax-free for our clients as possible.

I often ask the audience at my seminars, "What's worse than having money subject to tax?"

"Not having any money," I answer for them. They usually nod in approval, because it is true. While we groan about paying taxes, they are a part of our society. We do our best to maneuver your money so it exists in a tax-free realm; but, at the end of the day, we all must pay taxes.

Paying taxes means you are making money. I tell my audience, "I am going to pass a hat around, and everyone should put in all the money they want, and I will pay taxes on however much I receive. I am okay with that." It means I am making money.

The big question, of course, is deciding how to arrange your finances to keep the toll at a minimum. Every individual's tax circumstances are different, and robust retirement planning takes that into account. A one-size-fits-all answer does not exist.

Some brokers may suggest that spending taxable assets first is a good idea, that riding your IRA until you are seventy is the best approach. But in most cases, that's insane. A bigger IRA withdrawal above a certain level triggers a higher tax bill. This means paying more and getting less, certainly not what you hope for when you have already paid a fair share of taxable assets thus far. One of the toughest problems we tackle every spring is managing the "tax-hit" problem for folks having to take large RMDs (required minimum distributions) from their IRAs.

We have discussed opportunity costs in previous chapters. Paying taxes fits squarely into the conversation. Every dollar you spend on taxes is a dollar you do not have to spend on enjoying your retirement, whether it is taking a vacation or dedicating money to your grandkids' inheritance.

Other brokers may claim that investing in a 401(k), especially one in which an employer matches investments, is a dramatically better investment than an insurance policy. Maybe, but not necessarily. In fact, each and every dollar of your 401(k) account is subject to tax. On the other hand, life insurance distributions are tax-free. Consider this: a retirement plan that delivers $40,000 per year in income amounts to $28,000 after taxes. That's a significant difference. That $12,000 could be used for a cruise, or to invest in the money market.

The important thing to remember is that brokers will not always be forthcoming when it comes to the tax consequences of the investments they recommend—or they just don't know or care about them. It is up to the buyer—in this case the retiree—to beware. The most prudent thing to do is work with an advisor who can help steer you the right way using expertise and transparency. You have spent your working life paying taxes, and you will pay taxes in your retirement as well. But you should not find yourself in a situation where you pay more than your share, more than what is necessary. Taxes represent a threat to your wealth, but it is our duty, as your financial advisors, to remove the risk of paying unnecessary taxes due to poor planning.

In most cases, paying too much in taxes is not a crippling blow that happens at once. Rather, it happens slowly, year by year. Money slips through the cracks and, in the end, can amount to a small fortune. Human nature tells us to pay attention to the major events, that the big losses and huge gains warrant our attention, but with financial planning, success comes down to paying attention to the small stuff, the details, the seemingly minor decisions that turn out to have grave consequences. It's as simple as looking at the numbers. You will not feel the tax on a $2,000 investment nearly as much as when you take out $50,000 per year and have to pay $15,000 each time in taxes. It becomes not only a matter of when you take the money out, but how.

I have never had a client say, "I am glad I made the decision to pay more tax." It's never happened, and it never will. After all, saving money on taxes means more money in your pocket or portfolio.

In fact, your only taxable money should be what you intend to use for living expenses. That's the bottom line. Mistakenly, some retirees pay taxes on money that they turn around and reinvest, or they pull their minimum distributions and turn around and put them in taxable investments—in essence paying tax twice. Clearly, this is an instance of a retiree paying more than his fair share.

Keep this in mind: it is your right to take whatever tax breaks you can. It is not unpatriotic or wrong to take advantage of tax breaks. In fact, the government has an interest in promoting such tax-deductible investments as charitable giving and home ownership. But do not count on the government to share this information with you. It is up to the retiree to stay informed. With the proper financial guidance, retirees can save thousands in taxes, and do so in a way that is entirely congruent with their politics.

Three types of assets comprise a portfolio: taxable, tax-deferred, and tax-free. Tax-free includes municipal bonds, insurance products, Roth IRAS, 529 education accounts, and more. Tax-deferred assets include 401(k)s and traditional IRAS, tax-deferred annuities, and more. And finally, taxable assets usually include CDS, mutual funds, equities, and dividends.

Each asset type has a purpose and needs to be designed to deliver the maximum amount while paying the lowest amount of tax. Again, how that happens depends on an individual's circumstances. The important thing is to recognize the proper ways of avoiding overpaying in taxes and to understand how much a particular asset will be taxed when it is distributed. It is crucial that your advisor helps you weigh the advantages and disadvantages for every investment you own or are interested in obtaining.

Pensions have largely been replaced by 401(k)s; 401(k)s have never been more popular. But the harsh truth is that, because we are now at a historically low tax rate, we can expect to see higher rates in the near future. Higher tax rates are a threat to a retiree's wealth. Higher tax rates drain 401(k)s.

The message we have always heard is that even without a pension, the new or soon-to-be retiree can depend on his or her 401(k) or IRA, and that it will take care of them throughout retirement. They will be in a lower tax bracket by the time of retirement, and as such, they can expect to pay less in taxes. But if the tax rate is due to rise, and retirees are not in fact in a lower tax bracket, 401(k)s can be substantially diminished.

Questions arise about the most opportune time to withdraw money from a portfolio, and many factors play a part in making that decision. We are sure to examine thoroughly a client's portfolio and discuss his goals and lifestyle expectations. Based on this information, and how the client wishes to manage his money, we can make an educated strategy that ensures the client pays the minimum amount of tax. The government's required minimum distribution (RMD), though, keeps this strategy in check.

An RMD is an annual amount that must be withdrawn from a traditional IRA or a qualified retirement plan, such as a 401(k) or 403(b) after the account owner reaches the age of seventy-and-a-half years old. The last date allowed for the first withdrawal is April 1 following the year in which the owner reaches seventy-and-a-half. Some employer plans may authorize employees who are still employed to delay distributions until they stop working even if they are older than seventy-and-a-half.

RMDs are designed to ensure that owners of tax-deferred retirement plans do not defer paying taxes on their accounts year after year. Penalty-free distributions are allowed from tax-deferred retirement accounts after the person reaches age fifty-nine-and-a-half, but it is mandatory that the individual begin taking withdrawals by the time he reaches seventy-and-a-half. If a person delays taking his first distribution until April 1 following the year he turns seventy-and-a-half, he must use another distribution from his retirement portfolio that year. Annual RMDs must be taken each subsequent year no later than December 31.

The amount of a person's RMD depends on his age, the number in his portfolio, and his life expectancy. The IRS has a Uniform Lifetime Table that helps determine life expectancy.

To calculate RMD, divide the value of your account balance at the end of the previous year by the number of years you are expected to live based on the numbers generated by the IRS Lifetime Table. RMDs apply to each eligible account in a portfolio. If you do not take RMDs, you may be subject to a hefty 50 percent federal income tax penalty on the amount of the RMD. Conversely, the federal government issues various fees for early withdrawal. Both scenarios illustrate why it is important to discuss these matters with an advisor who can help manage and mitigate any issues that may arise. What's more, it is important to remember that distributions from tax-deferred retirement plans are subject to ordinary tax. Waiting until April 1 each year after reaching age seventy-and-a-half is a one-time option and requires that you take two RMDs in the same tax year. If these distributions are high, then you very well may be pushed into a higher tax bracket, a particularly grim scenario given that we now know that we can expect tax rates to increase in the future. The bottom line is to plan ahead and know what to expect.

Various types of iras exist. It is important and ultimately advantageous to understand the difference between each one. In the end, choosing an IRA, such as a Roth IRA, could wind up saving you money.

The following is an overview of IRAs that will help you uncover the differences between each type. At one time, there was little confusion about IRAs because only one kind existed. Now, however, various forms are in use, such as traditional IRAs, educational IRAs, and, of course, Roth IRAs.

Traditional IRAs are funded with deductible and non-deductible contributions, and you can enroll in them even if you are also in an employee-sponsored program. Deductible IRA contributions reduce a current tax bill overall, and earnings are deferred. However, every dollar withdrawn from the IRA is taxed. If you take money out before reaching age fifty-nine-and-a-half, penalties apply. The same goes for failing to reach RMDs once you reach age seventy-and-a-half. Traditional IRAs typically speak to high earners, or those looking to defer tax expenses up front. Bear in mind, tax-deferral, particularly IRAs, will prove to be the least efficient of all ways that you can accumulate funds for your retirement years.

Educational IRAS are savings accounts dedicated to a child's education. There is no deduction for contributions made to an educational IRA, and the earnings build up over time in a tax-deferred basis and are tax-free if the money is used for qualified expenses such as college.

The Roth IRA was enacted behind the leadership of Senator William Roth Jr. of Delaware, as a part of the Taxpayer Relief Act of 1997. Today, Roth IRAS are one of the most attractive assets in American retirement portfolios. Senator Roth envisioned the Roth IRA as a means to an end—a way to achieve the American Dream. In a Roth IRA, taxes are paid up front, but withdrawals are tax-free. This allows for a modest initial investment that can grow with compound interest over time and, when the money is withdrawn, avoid tax expenses. Roth IRAS are a sound way to build your portfolio. Over the years, they have gone through many changes and expansions, but today, they remain an attractive investment tool for young and old investors. Roth IRAS were designed for average investors, which means if you earn too much, you may be ineligible. However, portions of a salary can be converted and invested in a Roth IRA. Individual circumstances dictate whether converting to a Roth IRA is wise. But if you intend to be in a higher tax rate by the time you retire, converting your money—whether it is from a 401(k) or a traditional

IRA—to a Roth IRA could be a smart decision. We make it a policy to review with our clients all the options on the table. Most often, we recommend Roth IRAs, or Roth look-alikes, which essentially achieve the same thing.

HIDDEN FEES

Hidden fees, which we have already discussed, always pose a risk because they are, unfortunately, part of the investing game. It's crucial to be vigilant and look for hidden fees inside 401(k)s, mutual funds, and variable annuities. Personally, I like disclosure. I am an investment advisor who discloses all my fees. Others do not. Be sure to review thoroughly all documents before signing them. Too often, people come to me thinking they only pay a 0.5 percent fee, when in fact they pay 0.5 percent plus another 3 percent; the 3 percent portion is hidden.

LONGEVITY

The biggest, most fundamental risk, the one that all the others seem to play into, is the risk of longevity. People just might live too long. It soon might be common for people to live to 120 or even 130 according to some projections. If you think about that for a moment—the fear of longevity—you will see the irony. Isn't our primal fear supposed to be that we will die, not that we will keep living?

The problem with longevity risk is that it is a multiplier for additional risks—interest-rate risk, sequence-of-returns risk. Why? The longer we're living, the longer we are exposed to interest rate increases and burdensome sequence-of-returns rates. Longevity exacerbates the other risks we face. That includes long-term care and other healthcare costs. The longer we live, the more likely it is that we will need long-term care. Simply put: longevity increases other risks exponentially. But people most often do not want to think about it, and they certainly do not wish to purchase life insurance for when the time eventually does arrive. It's a tricky point to make that we are all going to die, but I make it merely to illustrate the importance of preparing for, and accepting, our end. Consider this: there is an 18 percent chance, over the next twenty years, that you will use auto insurance—and yet everybody driving a car has or is supposed to have auto insurance. There is a 3 percent chance that you will use homeowner's insurance, and yet the majority of homeowners have homeowner's insurance. People will pay insurance for something that may happen, but they are reluctant to pay for something that is inevitable. Investor behavior is once again at play here; it overrides rational thinking with speculative thought.

Some people enjoy the thrill of investing; it's in their nature. After all, people play the lottery; they gamble on the golf course and when they visit Las Vegas. It only makes sense that they take the same approach to investing. This holds true when discussing the portion of the population that has not saved much money, folks who typically earn high salaries but do not save much. These people are not good stewards of their wealth.

When it comes time to put their portfolios to work, they do not want a lifestyle change; rather, they are more likely to make risky investments under the mistaken impression that huge returns are only one smart stock pick away.

It happens all the time. People come to us with $500,000, but they want to take out $50,000 per year. I tell them they must not expect to live too long, because it's a plan that won't work. Sure, it'll do from ages sixty-five to seventy-five, but after that? Forget it. On the other side of the coin, people who have saved money and contributed to a retirement plan—as well as those who are fortunate enough to have pensions and are not crushed by debt—have great retirements.

Some readers may be familiar with the "Rule of 100." It's an oft-touted stock/bond mix that takes an investor's age and subtracts it from one hundred. Whatever that number is, that is the amount that should be invested in equities, stocks, mutual funds, and so on. The rest, whatever is left over, should be placed in something safe. The problem with the "Rule of 100" is that it does not discern between an aggressive and conservative investor. It does not take into account that everybody is different and has different circumstances and needs. It's easy to come up with a formula and put a bow on it—claiming it works for everyone. But that is not the case. The "Rule of 100" is used by many advisors, but it is a simple approach to complex, subjective matters. How we invest for our clients depends on their time frame. We segregate the buckets of money from conservative to aggressive based on time. We base all our decisions on when our clients need the cash. It seems to me that the "Rule of 100" was created to sell annuities. You will never see this rule discussed by planners—only insurance agents. Remember, if the only tool you have is a hammer, then everyone gets treated like a nail!

Unless retirees invest wisely and responsibly, a million-dollar nest egg can be depleted to a fraction of what it once was. But if you listen to the media and Wall Street, it's as if they want you to take the risk. After all, Wall Street wins whether you win or not. And keep in mind, as risk increases, the likelihood of success declines. Remember, market downturns occur regularly. It is only over the long term that the assets in the money market yield the steady returns needed for a lifetime of income. I am not into performance. You cannot eat or spend performance. You need money!

Short-term performance means nothing. Investing is a marathon, and, as I said in the introduction, you should not bother getting out of bed unless you are prepared to run the full twenty-six miles. We make sure we have a plan people adhere to; we plan before we invest, rather than the other way around, which is all too common.

CHAPTER 6

THE SOLUTION

INCOME FOR A LIFETIME

THIS CHAPTER FOCUSES ON HOW TO STRENGTHEN the third leg of the stool—your savings. Investing your portfolio so it provides a reliable income to cover essential and discretionary needs for the rest of your life is the challenge.

I have already shared some stories about new retirees who justify their lack of saving by saying that when they are older, toward the end of their retirement, they will not need the money they need now when they are still active. Many people who come to me are fortunate enough to have had high incomes. They've lived a luxurious lifestyle, traveled the world, eaten at the finest restaurants, and owned multiple homes. Their philosophy is they don't need to save too much money now, because later, when they are old and gray, they will not spend as much.

But as we saw in the last chapter, people are living longer, and healthcare costs are skyrocketing. The risks multiply, making the act of saving and looking at retirement realistically all the more important. Even the highest earners face the harsh reality of running out of money if they are not cautious about their spending habits and planning. The challenge is drawing income that can support a specific lifestyle. When retirees are forced to change their expectations, the sunny side of retirement grows dark quickly. I hate to be the bearer of bad news, but I also refuse to sell a client a fantasy. If the scenario above pertains to one of my clients, I tell them, "You will not have enough money to maintain your current lifestyle throughout your retirement."

Having an income for a lifetime means strengthening that third leg of the three-legged stool to provide a reliable income to cover essential needs and to meet your personal goals. We map this plan out for the rest of a client's life. We analyze spending habits and forecast tax, healthcare, and interest rates; we segregate the client's assets into the three buckets of income, liquidity, and legacy, and we maintain the levels of assets in those buckets to ensure the client is never without the cash he needs.

One way investors try to increase savings is to spend as little as possible on term insurance, thereby freeing up more money to invest. Using this method, they assume they can invest better than the insurance companies can in a cash-value insurance policy. While these investments occasionally bring home attractive returns, it is important to remember that even the best investors go broke now and then. As a new retiree, are you willing to run that risk? I am not, which is why I do not agree with this approach.

The problem is that life insurance is an estate planning tool, as well as a protection tool. It protects your ability to seize new opportunities and protect assets. It also passes money to the subsequent generations that follow you, and it ends up being timely and tax-efficient. The problem with term insurance is that only about 1 percent of the policy is written in the claim. The rest of the money that is converted to a permanent policy is usually dropped altogether. Personally, I don't have a problem with it—as long as people understand what they are doing.

But we like to take things a step further. We tell people, "Buy your income, and invest the difference." It's a poignant phrase that Curtis Cloke, creator of the Thrive Process, first said, and it's one that people remember. But what does it mean?

Buying your income means nothing more than taking some of your assets and creating an income, similar to an annuity or a bond ladder, or taking withdrawals from a CD. It means taking from a guaranteed investment or savings plan and generating income that is predictable, and hopefully, guaranteed. The idea is that this money lasts at least to a point in time when there are no longer any surprises; or, if there are, and you run out of money, another asset is waiting to take its place.

So, we understand the thought process of buying term insurance and investing the difference. We understand why some people might say, "I will just lock in my death benefit, but I will do it cheaply, so I can invest the difference."

Buy income and invest the rest.

It comes down to arriving at the minimum amount of revenue needed to cover fixed expenses. Let's say you are a new retiree with fixed costs at $2,000 per month. Fixed expenses include food, shelter, and automobile insurance—anything you pay for monthly that is necessary to living. When each month's fixed costs are added up, this amounts to the fixed number you need to spend every year. We encourage our clients—while using the least income possible—to make sure they cover their fixed expenses. But how do we do that? A variety of options exist, such as taking interest off of bonds on a bond ladder, a CD, or a moneymaking account. But in today's market, CDs and moneymaking accounts do not work well, because they barely beat out inflation. More and more, we turn to annuities, a fixed annuity of some kind that has what we call an income rider. The rider is the same thing you attach to the base policy that generates an amount of revenue, either today or in the future.

That's just one option. However you decide to do it, mainly the trick is finding a product to put your money into and then using as little income as possible to cover fixed expenses. This frees up the rest of your assets so you can be a bit more aggressive in investing in other areas. Ultimately, this is the same premise behind term insurance; if you pay less for insurance and it still protects you—takes care of the family in the case of death, for example—if that coverage is guaranteed and cheap, then there is more cash on hand to spend on other investments.

If an annuity can produce significant value, then it allows for investing more dollars and ultimately making more money. That's the goal. We make sure our clients have income that is going to last as long as they do. Since we do not know how long that is going to be, we have to make sure we err on the side of old age. We don't want the money to expire before they do.

Now, thinking in these terms sounds reasonable, but sometimes a client will not be able to see the advantage, or will not want to decrease the amount of money used as income. I had a couple attend one of my seminars; they liked what they heard and scheduled a meeting. They said they agreed with everything I had said and wanted to accomplish what I had discussed in the seminar. They had made some mistakes in the past, but they were high earners, so it would be all right, they said. Bottom line: they did not want to run out of money.

The husband, Dwight, had a base income of $250,000 per year. On top of that, most years, he received a bonus anywhere from $50,000 to $90,000. Dwight and his wife, Gina, traveled the world; he had a company expense account and a company car. They moved to Hilton Head when Dwight, at sixty-six, was preparing for retirement.

Despite Dwight's high earnings, he and Gina had little in assets. All told, they had maybe $750K, which, of course, is still substantial. But when you factor in the amount of money they made during Dwight's career years and the lifestyle it afforded them, $750K would not suffice in retirement—especially if you follow the 4 percent withdrawal strategy.

Four percent of $750,000 is $30,000 per year. Dwight had Social Security but no pension. He and Gina would be slipping from a quarter-million dollars per year to $30K with no job and more time to spend money. And remember, when he was working, he was not spending as much, primarily owing to the company car and expense account. Even if we add in $30,000 in Social Security, the numbers do not hold up. They began to see the deficiencies in their portfolio. They discussed how much they could save if Dwight were to work for another five years. They thought roughly $2,500 per month, $30,000 annually. In five years that is $150,000 plus growth—I could make it work. I told them so.

But Gina wanted Dwight at home, so he decided he would retire at sixty-six. So that $150,000 was never deposited into their bank account.

I said, "Look, you guys can't retire at this level. You can retire if you want to retire, of course, but you need to understand what your deficiencies are."

They began justifying their position the same way I have heard it explained by many others, that they had already had the chance to do the things they wanted to do. In retirement, there would be less spending, not more. As such, they could retire now, pull the income they wished, and make money on investments.

Dwight and Gina remained our clients for another year, but when the reality of their financial situation settled in, they needed someone to blame. They complained that our equity accounts had not made enough. But during those years, nobody's equity accounts did very well. They thought they could make more. They left us. I wished them well but knew they would run out of money. It wasn't a question of if, but when. After all, retirees spend a different amount of money during various parts of their retirement.

I will not participate in a client's misguided approach or assist them in certain failure. Again, it comes back to chemistry, goals, worth, and value. Retirement can be broken down in ten-year increments. The first ten years are the go-go years. During this period, you feel great; you're newly retired! You are as young as you ever will be and want to do the things you never could do before while you were busting your hump working for a living. So, you are touring, on cruises, flying to distant destinations. And don't forget the grandkids and golf—all in all, life is good.[3]

Then you enter the second period, right around seventy-five to eighty—the slow-go years. You can still do all the things you used to do, but you just don't want to anymore—or not as much. You don't want to kayak three times per week. You don't want to drive to Jacksonville to play golf. Hence, you are not spending the money you once were. Essentially, things have slowed down. You're not infirm with health issues; it's just that you do not wish for so much activity anymore.[4]

Finally, when you are somewhere near eighty-five, you have the no-go years. During this period, poor health typically curtails most traveling and physical activity. It's not that you no longer have the inclination to do certain things; it is that you cannot physically do them. By this point, most people are not spending much more than their pension, Social Security dollars, and Medicare dollars. Some people say their family members

3   Tom Hegna, *Don't Worry, Retire Happy! Seven Steps to Retirement Security*, Wellington, New Zealand: Tross Press, 2014.
4   Ibid.

live into their hundreds; others say their family members live only into their seventies. Either way, each group wants to adjust their spending accordingly. But there are no rules regarding longevity. So, we always prepare for a long life while adhering to the three ten-year periods of retirement.[5]

One time, at a seminar, a man raised his hand and said, "Hey, I want my last check to bounce. Can you make that happen?"

I said, "Sure. Just tell me what year you're going to die. That's the only information I need."

The audience chuckled at that one, but it is the truth. I have never had a client say, "I have two goals in life. The first is I want to die, and the second is I want to die quickly." But if you spend your retirement assets unwisely, the only way to recoup the loss is to die and quickly. Now, I know that is a harsh way of putting things in perspective, but I don't like beating around the bush. The point of everything we do is to think about it wholly and realistically. If a client only wants a quick answer that suits his position on one item, then he needs to find a different advisor. We deliver the total package, not pieces of it. And the whole package means income for life.

The bottom line is that traditional income plans, ones that follow the market, work when the market is up, but markets also go down. When they do, if you depend on that money, you're

---

5   Ibid.

in trouble. An income plan should and can work in all markets, good, bad, and sideways.

The goal is to develop a lifetime income and identify growth opportunities that, over time, get you back to the amount of your original principal. Of course, you will have set expenses and discretionary expenses, and on top of that, inflation is a concern. As we discussed, we can move assets to accomplish specific goals and set up income for the long term. It's important to rely on guaranteed returns in the short term and be in the market for higher returns in the long term, say fifteen to twenty-five years, while still hedging against inflation.

A sound retirement plan must provide a proper balance of safety, so income is guaranteed. The plan must consist of liquidity, so that cash is accessible in emergencies, and of growth so that retirees can outrun inflation. Finally, the plan must grow the portfolio to replenish income needs and perhaps leave an inheritance.

A "perfect storm" has emerged comprising low-interest rates, volatile stock markets, and unprecedented longevity. These realities are sure to create stress for many retirees as they seek ways to make their retirement income last as long as they do.

More than ever before, retirees are dependent upon their investments to generate retirement income. With fewer companies providing traditional pension plans, retirees are being forced to assume the investment risk associated with their retirement assets.

Of course, widespread uncertainties about the future of Social Security continue to linger. Increasing budget deficits and financial uncertainty only serve to create additional anxiety for retirees. All of these factors combine in a way that causes retirees to seek investment choices that offer safety but also provide growth opportunities to meet their income needs for both today and tomorrow.

Until now, no asset allocation approach was available that placed sufficient emphasis on the present and future income needs of retirees. The central objective of the "Income Bliss" model is to provide an inflation-adjusted income for life.

The proper balance of safety, liquidity, and growth is different for each retiree. Some risk is appropriate and unavoidable, specifically with money markets and other growth opportunities. But how much each retiree can tolerate depends on the retiree's individual circumstances, such as age, health, family, and more. In the next chapter, we will uncover the vital steps to securing retirement income. We will ask fundamental questions, beginning with, "What is the difference between how much I will need each month and how much I will have?"

CHAPTER 7

STEPS TO SECURE RETIREMENT INCOME

2 x 3 x 10 x 7 x 52 x 20.

WHAT DO YOU SUPPOSE THOSE NUMBERS MEAN? In sum, they amount to $436,800.

2 x 3 x 10 x 7 x 52 x 20 = $436,800.

That's how much it costs two retirees to eat for twenty years. Look closely: two people, eating three times per day, with each meal costing ten dollars, for seven days per week, fifty-two weeks per year, over the course of twenty years.

$436,800.

Staggering. And ten dollars a meal is low. (I have tried to do this, but while you can save by skipping breakfast or having a banana—one night on the town blows your averages!) I use this number to illustrate, to drive home why retirement planning is so hard and expensive and, if left unattended, stressful. What's more, the $436,800 is after tax. Taxes were paid on the money that purchased that food. In the end, the sum is even more, close to $525,000. This gives us a sense of why it takes so much money to retire.

Chapter 6 addressed the ways we help clients strengthen the third leg of the stool—your savings—using a practice we call "buy your income and invest the rest." We now understand that in order to successfully generate income for life, a plan must provide liquidity, safety, and growth.

But what happens when a client's assets are not substantial enough to maintain their desired lifestyle? Moreover, the key question clients need to answer is the difference between how much they will need each month and how much they have in savings, the money market, bonds, and so on. After all, a plan only works if capital exists to propel it forward. We can deliver the most pristine, thorough plan known to man, but unless the client has the means to support it—and wishes to generate income for life, not just income for now—the capital needs to be made available.

Answering these questions requires math and the absence of emotion. Emotion, whether it is linked to aggressive investor behavior or timid nonaction, seriously hampers financial planning. If we move too aggressively, we carry more risk. We want to minimize risk, not maximize it. If we are too timid and do not seize new opportunities, assets may dry up, thwarting growth.

So, let's assume we've removed emotion from our decision-making process. We are left with math. The first thing we need to look at is how much the client has in his portfolio. Many times, people will come to see me with what they consider a robust portfolio, but they do not have a clue how much money retirement requires.

We return to the fundamental question of how much a retiree needs versus how much he has. At this point, we need to uncover his income sources, how long he will need them, and what he needs to pay for first. We size up his goals, individual needs, and resources.

Often, a client comes to us with a certain amount of assets. He wants us to build a plan that uses his pension (if he has one), Social Security, and assets. He wants us to identify his shortcomings, but also provide a road map for income that supports his desired lifestyle. If it were that easy, I'd be a lot happier, because it would mean everybody would have enough money to live the kind of retirement they want. But it's not the case, unfortunately.

Roughly 60 percent of the people I see are shocked by how much money it takes to retire. Now that we know how much it costs to eat, we also must consider that correlated with living longer lives (longevity rears its ugly head!) are the costs of long-term healthcare. The average male, if he reaches sixty-five, has a 50 percent probability of living to age eighty-five or longer. The average female has a 50 percent probability of living to age eighty-eight. There is a 50 percent chance, between two sixty-five-year-old people, that one will live to ninety-two. And finally, there is a 25 percent chance of one living to ninety-seven and a 5 percent chance of one living to one hundred years old. Long story short: you must prepare for a long retirement.

If you make less than $170,000 per year and live to the average life expectancy, the cost of insurance, Medicare, and copay amounts to roughly $256,000 for the total length of retirement. On top of that, add the out-of-pocket costs for medications and other health-related expenses. That's close to $100,000 in most cases, bringing our total to nearly $400,000. Add that to the cost of meals, and we are looking at $900,000 just for going to the doctor and eating food during retirement. We're not including trips, new air conditioners, cars, or gifts and money for the children and grandkids. Again, these numbers are not designed to intimidate, or instill a sense that all is lost; rather, this is to impress upon our clients just how much money they can plan on spending. That is why when clients like Dwight and Gina visit us—high earners with low net worth—the planning proves especially difficult and almost always ends in failure. Many people want a planner who tells them everything is okay, even if it's not. We don't do that.

Occasionally, we have a client who has been fortunate enough to earn a high income and wise enough to invest and save over the years. Recently, a client visited and said, "Bob, I need $100,000 per year in income. We've saved $3,000,000. My wife and I have Social Security at $35,000 per year; I have a pension for $20,000 annually." With all the costs tallied, that leaves us with a shortfall of $45,000. But we can build a plan for this couple and still have money left over for their legacy interests.

Another couple came in recently for legacy planning. They had $100,000 per year from their pension fund, and they lived quite modestly. We moved some assets into their legacy funds, and they started planning what they wished to leave for their grandkids. This couple has the luxury of a robust pension, healthy savings, and a modest lifestyle, which allows them to enjoy an income for life and still leave a beautiful gift to their grandkids.

These examples are exceptions, unfortunately. Typically, we hear situations closer to the husband and wife with $200,000 in a brokerage account, an IRA worth $190,000, and other income of $30,000 to $50,000 per year. That's an average client. It's not a home run of a portfolio, and indeed, some lifestyle changes may need to occur, but the bottom line is, we make the plan work. Regardless of the circumstances, if clients have realistic expectations and have done their job of saving and investing wisely, we make the plan work. We solve their problem so they can enjoy retirement.

There are two issues we encounter when we start to plan for a retiree's income, but they usually depend on how the client plans to use her money. Income planning can be based on interest rates. For example, say a client has $1,000,000, and for the money they need currently, they need a 1 percent return for five years. For the subsequent six to ten years, they need a 3 percent return. And finally, once we get to ten, fifteen, twenty years out, they need returns at 7 percent. Obviously, that money is in the stock market. Over time, markets are efficient. Live with the down years, because there are years to offset the losses. This is one example of how we build a plan.

We'd also have a plan that incorporates mistakes, and ensuring money is set aside to make up for them. We have a plan that covers longevity, of course, and one that plans for legacy giving. Again, it depends on the client's circumstances and wishes.

Some advisors try to improve the numbers. But the only way they can do it is by taking on high risk and not planning for the long term. Some advisors plan for fifteen years instead of thirty years. Looking at the higher returns, the client, in this case, might be elated. But the returns only forecast for a limited time—fifteen years. What happens if the client lives to ninety? They won't run out of money entirely, of course, because of Social Security and other residual sources of income, but they will run out of something else: lifestyle.

People often warn about running out of money, and even in this book, I have said that an unrealistic financial plan threatens a retiree's well-being. The clients we typically engage with have money, they have earned and saved, so they are never going to run out of money entirely, but they will lose their lifestyle if they enter retirement unprepared. For people who are used to a way of life, such news comes as a shock. Nobody wants to sell the beach house, but sometimes the circumstances warrant it.

In most cases, I say to the client, "Look, you might live past the age of ninety or you might not. If you do not, we have plenty of money. We can discuss planning your legacy. But if you do live past ninety, we need a plan B. We need emergency cash."

Typically, we will plan the "Income Bliss" model for thirty years, or at least to age ninety. Within it, we have a recovery segment. The recovery segment puts aside enough money that is set at a certain rate of return. Keep in mind that we have a twenty-five-year window in which we can be a bit more aggressive with those assets than we would be during a five- or ten-year period. At any rate, I ask the client how much money she would like to have in her portfolio twenty-five years from now.

Most don't know; they do not know how much they will need. As our parents taught us, most people are conditioned to live on interest and never invade principal. We encourage the same thing. We tell people it's in their best interest to have a plan that keeps principal sacrosanct. If they agree, and I build a plan, I typically suggest that we strive to have at least the same amount in the portfolio twenty-five years later as they did when they entered retirement. But what happens over the course of twenty-five years? The principal deflates. If you have $1 million, sometimes that reduces to as little as $500,000. Half a million dollars is better than zero dollars, but even that only holds true while protecting principal.

To protect the principal on a million dollars, the client needs guaranteed investments. For example, imagine the client could get 3 percent returns (that's very hard, but let's assume it is true). That's $30,000 per year. Imagine saving $1 million, but because you wish to protect the principal, only $30,000 is available. That's not a rosy picture. Most people don't accept such a small number. They cannot live on it. Even if we followed the traditional route and lived off interest, the rates are too low. The same applies to CDs. CDs once had rates at 10 percent, but no longer. If that were the case, you could just put a quarter of a million dollars in different banks, $100,000 in each, take the interest, and there you go, happy as a clam. But alas, that's a fantasy in today's world. We did see 10 percent rates in the

1980s, and it will eventually happen again, but with high interest rates comes high inflation—a double-edged sword.

As we learned in the last chapter, with high inflation, the population loses its purchasing power. However, even if you do not spend copious amounts of money, are a somewhat frugal retiree, and don't owe significant sums of debt, getting 10 percent is an extraordinary situation. But those days are not returning anytime soon; just look at our Treasury. We cannot afford our national debt, and we cannot pay the interest on it, and because our debt is predicated on our Treasury, we see interest at 1 to 2 percent.

The same thing goes for bonds. We have a great tendency to forget what a bond is. A bond is nothing more than an entity that loans money. That entity pays interest in return for people buying the bond, essentially lending it money. If the entity is paying a certain amount of interest, and then that interest increases, that drains the entity's capital or reserves. Nonetheless, I'd love to see interest rates increase to 3 to 5 percent at least—then I'd be willing to take the traditional route and for a time, use interest for income.

That's why we do something different. That's why we segregate assets into income buckets, because I am then able to demonstrate different ways to take in more money. But to identify different ways of making more money, I need to understand how much risk a client is willing to take. I have said before that we are risk-averse. But once we have the client's money broken into buckets, and we know how much we have to work with at any given time, then we can take a bit more risk with the money that won't be touched for more than ten, fifteen, or twenty years.

A good planner does not inflate the numbers he presents to his clients. A good planner provides realistic numbers that prepare for the long term. If I have a client with a million dollars, and I have broken his money into buckets that span five, ten, fifteen, and twenty years, the next thing I need to understand is how much risk is acceptable. Risk tolerance changes with personality. If you are optimistic, you might be willing to risk more, unlike the pessimistic person who prefers to risk less. Very few people have the same risk tolerance over time. Much of it depends on how the market performs and what is happening in their lives.

Once a level of risk is determined, we assign a moniker to the money; it's either red money or green money. Red money is money the client can afford to lose. Green money is safe money. The more money a client has, the more money he can afford to lose—if he is willing to take risks. If a client has a million dollars and wants access to $100,000, that's green money. That's liquid, and we put that money in the bank. It's accessible and waits for a rainy day. But ask a client how much money he can afford to lose, and always you will hear zero. Ask a client how much money he can afford to risk, and it ranges—10, 20, 40 percent of the money. That's red money.

However, let's stay with the example of the client with a million dollars with $100,000 on hand, and who is willing to risk, say, 40 percent of his money, so $400,000, in the market. Now we are at half a million. At this point, the green money becomes the difference between what we have already allocated and what we have left. To me, green money means guaranteed money. And this can come from all sources including Social Security, a pension, or anything that is dependable and does not decrease. I even like to take things a step further by using any gains I earn on green money and making them part of the subsequent year's principal. If I make 5 percent on $1 million, so $50,000, I aim to affix that to the $1 million principal. The ultimate goal with green money is latching on to an income strength that we cannot leave.

There are two things to solve before it is possible to settle on an appropriate income level. First, we must know when the client needs the money. If I have a client who does not want any money in equities, that client will have security but also a lower distribution rate on his retirement income. The problem, in this case, is that with no money in equities, the possibilities of earning diminish drastically. Usually, a client is swayed by how little money he will receive. Sometimes, the client has already lost money in the market and does not want to lose more, and so he remains inactive. I try to counsel in these cases that the client does not need all the money for thirty years. Some of it, of course, he needs, and that stays safe as green money. But the rest of it can be put on the market and invested a little more aggressively. If we are planning for a thirty-year retirement, being aggressive has nothing to do with how old you are; it's about the time frame and when you need the money.

Second, we need to know how that money will be accessed. The time frame is stationary, but the ways in which a client draws money are not. Money moves from bucket to bucket depending on circumstances, but no matter what, we always keep the end goal in mind. If it's to protect a one-million-dollar principal or to double that principal, that's what we strive to do, and we manage the money accordingly.

In summary, the first step in securing retirement income is to answer the fundamental question of how much money the client needs versus how much the client has. Once identified, it is time to discuss goals, individual needs, and resources. We need to find out how much money the client wants to meet essential expenses. Furthermore, we must know exactly how much the client needs to meet life goals.

With this information in hand, it is time to discuss risk. How much is the client willing to accept in the market? How much could his portfolio tolerate and still meet its essential purposes? We strive to take on as little risk as possible while still meeting the target rate of return.

Next, we set up investment priorities and allocate money accordingly in various portfolio accounts: one is for short-term spending needs and living expenses, and typically covers the first five years of retirement. This is safe, available money—green money.

The next segment we dedicate to longer-term needs covering the fifth to the tenth year of retirement. This segment is less liquid and invested for a higher rate, but it still relies on safe investments. As the short-term allocation empties, this segment replenishes it.

How we segment after ten years depends on the client's age and goals. Typically, the later segments are growth segments that take on more risk and go after higher returns in the long term with the goal of getting back the client's original principal.

It all comes down to this: the sooner you need money, the less risk you can accept. You can take more risk for the money you will not need for several years. You can take even more risk on money not needed for many years, if ever.

After all, if you have money you do not need for twenty-five years, you can invest it as aggressively as a forty-year-old. The market is typically very efficient in the long term.

Remember, circumstances change all the time, but one thing stays the same: the need for income, liquidity, and legacy. With these in place, your financial plan gives you money to live your ideal life. We help you achieve that ideal.

YOUR ESTATE, YOUR LEGACY

WHAT DOES YOUR LIFE MEAN? HOW DO YOU WANT your friends and family to remember you? What is important to you? What would you like to leave behind as a representation of how you spent your time on planet Earth?

These are tough questions, but they are important to answer. We all have an idea of who we are and what we stand for. Many of us are dedicated to the arts or our church. Others find community among college alumni or social clubs. The issue is not what you believe; the issue, for our purposes, is how you plan to design your legacy in financial terms. Charitable giving is a wonderful gesture. You do not need me to tell you the impact it can have on people and foundations in need. Outside of the altruistic nature of charitable giving, though, is a financial incentive.

Most people, once we resolve what their goals are for their money, look to charitable giving as a way for their memory to live on after they're gone. It's an important topic to discuss as you begin to evaluate your long-term goals. This chapter will highlight some of the most important talking points, and it will emphasize the importance of estate planning overall.

CHARITY: A WISE CHOICE

As an advisor, I encourage charitable giving because of its tax advantages. If you donate money to a charity in your will, your heirs can receive back the taxes you paid on that money, after you pass away. But there is much more to giving than the financial incentive. My wife and I, for example, prefer to give to local charities only. The fact that these charities are in our community makes the act and the benefit that much more immediate. But that is just us; it's the way we do things. At WSG, it's different. We support five charities that are near and dear to us. I will only mention one: JDRF. My youngest daughter was diagnosed with type 1 diabetes at age seven and has lived successfully with this awful disease for twenty years. My wife and I want to help find a cure for this dread disease, and we donate our time, energy, and financial resources to do so. There are hundreds of wonderful charitable organizations to donate your social capital to; please do so!

How do you want to be remembered? Again, this is a tough question. Many people do not wish to answer. Sometimes, it's because they are scared to look deep inside themselves, since they do not know what they will find. Other times, it's because answering the question forces the person to take action. That people would rather not make decisions is something I have learned over the years. People prefer to let things ride. But there is power in a decision and negative consequences in indecision. People tend to make more wrong decisions due to indecision than they do if they just move forward and make a decision, whether right or wrong. Most successful people make decisions very quickly. Leadership requires it.

Of course, we are not going to force a client into this discussion, but it happens to come up when we get around to discussing goals. The legacy bucket fills with everything not needed for liquidity and income; it's as simple as that.

I always ask my clients, "Would you like the ability to spend all your retirement assets and still be able to leave it all to your heirs?" Of course, each person I ask says yes, but how can it be done? The answer is life insurance.

We're always looking for the most economical way of having money in the legacy bucket. For us, that means life insurance. When a client has life insurance, his circle of wealth grows. We are able to return his principal back to its original amount, and, in essence, he can spend his retirement assets while increasing the amount in his legacy bucket over time. The fact of the matter is that it does not cost the client anything to provide a lasting legacy for their children, grandchildren, and the charity of their choice.

For example, you can have money coming from a life insurance policy distribution that still has a benefit at the time of your death. You can accomplish things with that. Many times, in fact, we will carve out the legacy bucket outside of the "Income Bliss" model, stopping us from having to delve into those precious funds that keep us safe. Money moves from bucket to bucket depending on circumstances and goals. The crucial thing is to keep the buckets balanced and to work toward the overall plan of income for life.

For example, a client's mother passed away recently at age ninety-six—a pretty good run, I'd say. Now, the family has a home to sell, and the mother had $300,000 on top of that. But my client does not need the money. He wants to donate it. He is quite frugal and knows they will not need the cash. They have roughly $2,000,000 in an IRA. That's not an astronomical amount, but because they are frugal and smart with their investments, they do not need it.

If you think about that—someone who is ninety-six has $300,000 in an IRA—it makes you wonder: How much did she once have? By the time you turn ninety-six, you have to take out 10, 15, 20 percent of that IRA because of the RMD. She must have had a large amount to begin with or lived frugally.

At any rate, the family wishes to donate money to their church and local college. To accommodate this, we set up a charitable remainder trust (CRT). Using a CRT, we named the college as the recipient, which means that the college receives everything that is left after the IRA pays its direct beneficiary. A CRT allows you to gift an asset. In turn, you increase income, receive a tax deduction, and at the time of death, whatever is left in the asset goes to the charity. So, what have you achieved? You have eased your tax burden, taken care of your income, and, at your demise, provided your charity with an excellent sum.

Here is another way to look at it. Imagine you have a valuable piece of artwork. Say it is valued at $100,000. You love to look at it in your home, but as an asset, it is not generating a dollar's worth of income. Sure, the art looks beautiful on your wall, and it may increase in value over time, but unless you activate the art by selling it or donating it, it is not going to provide income.

Now, say you have this artwork, and you are looking for a way to help your favorite charity but cannot figure out a way to do it. That's when I ask, "What about your artwork?"

The client always says, "But we love it; we love looking at it."

And that may be true. After all, I enjoy art as much as the next person.

"But what if we could do more good with it?" I ask. "Would you be willing to take a look at another opportunity?"

Here is how it happens.

Art is a non-income-producing asset. But if you give it to charity, you receive in return a significant tax break. Let's say it's 20 percent. That's a $20,000 tax break as a result of donating the art, a non-income producing asset, to charity. On the other hand, if you gave away an income-producing asset, you would lose the money it generated. Artwork, then, is dynamic in this regard. If the owner of the artwork sold it to another individual, the seller would have to pay taxes on the sale price, and they would not get back what they paid for it initially. On the other hand, if the owner gifts it to charity, they get a tax write-off, and then the charity can sell the art without having to pay taxes. When the church sells the art, they can then pay the original owner, through the CRT that's set up, an income of $5,000 per year for as long as they live. When the person dies, the remainder of the asset belongs to the charity.

It is plain to see why a CRT is a beneficial arrangement for charities and individuals alike. Now take a step back. What did we just do? The owner of the artwork did not need it hanging on his wall anymore. When he donated it to charity, he created a legacy.

It goes back to what we say to each of our clients: the perfect financial plan gives you the money to live your ideal life. The perfect plan has enough liquidity to take advantage of opportunities and pay for unforeseen situations; it has enough income to pay for your day-to-day living expenses; and it provides funds to pass along in your legacy, which will make a difference in the lives of the people you care about. Charitable giving, whether it is through artwork or cash, offers incentives for the giver and the recipient. Also, it does not relinquish control of your assets when you're gone; rather than the government collecting taxes and distributing your assets as they see fit, you keep control over exactly who benefits from your life's work.

I want my clients to enjoy their lives. I cannot make them do that, of course, but from a fiscal position, I can. I want to build a plan that works—that has the three components of income, liquidity, and legacy. I want to work with people who wish to leave a legacy. That is important to me. I not only want my clients to live an ideal life, but I also want them to leave behind something good. It's hard to arrive at that point, sometimes, because people are unsure how to go about planning for a time when they are not here, but if we can remove emotion from the equation, we arrive at the conclusion that charitable giving comes with financial incentives as well as altruistic ones.

ESTATE PLANNING

Now it is time to discuss estate planning. The words "estate" and "planning" can mean various things, but for our purposes, they suggest developing a plan designed to assist the loved ones who handle your estate when you are gone. This helps transfer assets from one generation to the next. Estate planning involves the use of a vital document—a will. A will registers a person's wishes regarding the distribution of his assets after death. A will is only applicable upon death. More elements go into estate planning, though, and for practical purposes, I will review them here.

Organize Paperwork

While making a will and implementing other estate planning strategies are necessary steps to take, many people overlook the issue of organizing this information in a way that is easy for family members to understand and handle. It is important to make sure your heirs are aware of their roles in your estate planning, and that they know how to access key documents.

As we all know, the grief associated with the passing of a loved one can be overwhelming. It is compounded when the relative leaves unorganized paperwork. But it does not need to be that way.

Be sure to organize information about wills and trusts. For each will and trust, include the following information:

- Document title
- Date prepared
- Effective date (e.g., upon incapacity)
- Attorney's name and contact information
- Location of documents
- Executor or Successor/Alternate

Durable Power of Attorney for Finances

A durable power of attorney remains valid after you are incapacitated and unable to manage your affairs. These powers cease upon death. After death, your will identifies who has the authority to control your affairs. For durable power of attorney, include the following:

- Document titles
- Date prepared
- Agent's name and contact information
- Effective date
- Attorney's name and contact information
- Location of documents

Insurance

Include insurance policies that you own as well as those of others that cover your life or property. This information is helpful to your executor or agent. List the following:

- Type of policy
- Policy number
- Insurance company
- Policy owner
- Description of coverage
- Location of policy

Bank and Brokerage Accounts

Your executor will need this information to contact financial institutions to arrange account access. For each bank or brokerage account, list the following:

- Financial institution names and contact information
- Description of assets
- Account number
- Specifics on death beneficiary transfers
- Cards, passwords, and online access
- Location of checkbook and statements

Retirement Plans, IRAs, and Pensions

The company or advisors managing your IRAS, retirement plans, and pensions will need to be notified upon death. Include the following information:

- Company name and contact information
- Description of assets
- Account number
- Beneficiary name and contact information
- Online access, statements, and passwords

Miscellaneous

Those are the primary documents to prepare, but it is also important to list information about healthcare, real estate, government benefits, and business holdings. The most important thing is to think comprehensively, to account for all of your assets, so it is simple for the handler to move through the information effectively.

Communicate about Your Estate Plan

The bottom line is that everyone has an estate plan, whether you realize it or not. In fact, you either have an estate tax problem or an estate size problem. Rest assured the government has an estate plan for you, although it is most likely not the plan you would choose. There are central concerns when it comes to estate planning. Most often people want to make sure their estates are properly managed if they are incapacitated or die. They want to ensure their estate is passed on to their loved ones, and not eaten by taxes or other charges. With this in mind, it is crucial to arrange assets to minimize tax costs and fees. A qualified advisor will guide you through this process, as difficult as it may be.

It is a good idea to start your estate planning while you are healthy; that way you have a level playing field. It is a good idea to communicate with your heirs what your desires are, so they can maintain the legacy you have put into place in a manner that is in step with your philosophy and goals.

After you have had discussions with your heirs and organized your relevant documents, it is time to devise a plan to maintain control of your assets even after you are gone. How?

A will is one answer, but that requires the estate to go through probate and does not control certain issues of the estate. Probate is the legal process that recognizes the authenticity of a will and names the representative who will manage the estate. Going through probate can be costly, however, and privacy issues can arise. It is recommended to work with an attorney.

The alternative to keeping a will is a living trust. A living trust allows you to sidestep probate and all its inherent costs and challenges, passing assets such as insurance payments, retirement plan proceeds, real estate holdings, and more on to your named beneficiary. Living trusts can have tremendous value in estate planning. Because we are living longer, a living trust works to curtail disagreements or misuse of an elderly loved one's assets—a crucial consideration when mapping out your estate plan. There are many more points to consider when setting up a living trust, but it is a viable means to enact a fair and sensible financial legacy.

A LEGACY IS YOUR STORY

In closing, it is important to remember that in leaving a legacy, it is not all about the money. It is just as much about passing on your values, ethics, and the story of who you are and what you believe. As I mentioned earlier, I very much want to work with people who share this sentiment, people who wish to make the world a better place. After all, there should be a point to our lifetime of work.

With your financial goals identified and planned for, with tax considerations and unforeseen costs anticipated, it is time to move onward. To live your ideal life, stop worrying about your financial outlook, and enjoy your retirement on your terms with loved ones by your side.

In this chapter, we have discussed the importance of estate planning and reviewed some of the benefits of charitable giving. As this book aims to provide an overview of these issues, I recommend coming in to see us to discuss these matters in greater detail. In the following chapter, we will look one last time at the themes addressed in this book, drive home the major points, and reiterate why good financial advice is so crucial to a happy retirement.

CHAPTER 9

ONWARD TO YOUR DREAMS

I WOULD LIKE TO CONCLUDE THIS BOOK WITH AN OVER-view of the points we have covered, and to hone in on how those points coalesce into an action-oriented plan for retirement. I will then pivot the focus toward what lies ahead—a retirement designed to deliver income for life, so you can draw the most from the days and experiences yet to come.

A primary concern for people approaching retirement is making sure they have enough money to last for the rest of their days. This matter does not change if you are a millionaire or live paycheck to paycheck. It is a primal fear that affects us all. We now know, however, that with proper planning, people entering the retirement phase can enjoy income for life. Making sure you have income for life is not easy, and it takes work, but it is achievable. In fact, we do it every day for our clients. We understand, now, that retirement is a new phase, unlike any experienced before. New retirees are different than their former selves, the people they were at work, so it is important to discuss early on how to spend time and maximize assets. After all, the rules have changed. The focus for the new retiree is no longer on accumulating money, but on protecting it.

We have discussed opportunity costs and how they are inherent in each and every dollar you spend. As an advisor, it is my job to provide advice on which opportunities are optimal, and which bear too heavy a cost. Remember, an opportunity cost is present in every investment, be it a new home, a mutual fund, or a charitable donation. It is essential to understand just how important opportunity costs are. They should be central to every decision made while planning for retirement. We are not here to control your life, but we do want you to delegate certain responsibilities to us, so you can enjoy your time. Opportunity costs are a sticking point for us—we consider them from all angles and encourage our clients to do the same.

This book makes it clear that I am not looking to do business with clients who are only after the highest returns, or who want to spend their time comparing benchmarks and performances.

Since this is a book of investment advice, and sound advice depends on an individual's circumstances, I have avoided doling out typical "beat the market" schemes or other hackneyed advice. I hope this book finds readers who recognize the need for professional advice, and people who realize they need help pulling together the many elements of a comprehensive retirement plan. When we build a retirement plan based on the "Income Bliss" model, we intend to ride the market slowly and only with a portion of the money the client can afford. We intend to cover short-term costs as well as projected long-term costs. We intend to adhere to the plan, so the client achieves his goals and expectations.

We are boring; we predicate our investments on dependability and conservative spending, which means we are not the right firm for everyone. Nor are we trying to be. Our goal is to work with clients who share our philosophy. In the end, the way we work develops stronger relationships and generates improved financial rewards. We base our philosophy on trust. Our clients trust us with their money, and we trust our clients—who ultimately have the final say—to adhere to our recommendations. We believe in winning by not losing. If a client has saved money, it is entirely possible to have an enjoyable, fruitful retirement without taking too much risk. As they say, "Moderate gains that never experience loss will outperform a volatile market over time."

We design financial plans up front, and we expect allegiance and adherence to them. We expect allegiance because by the time we develop a plan, the client has agreed with our philosophies and approach. We are methodical and proactive in our approach. There are no surprises.

In essence, we tailor plans for the individual. Each retiree has unique goals and dreams, risk tolerance, and day-to-day needs. It is up to us as advisors to tailor plans that meet, within reason, the expectations of our clients. We do this by truly getting to know our clients. I consider many of my longtime clients good friends. They are people who tend to be fifty-five years old or older, have legitimate to substantial assets in their portfolios, and are either already retired or soon-to-be retired.

In each chapter presented in this book, I have attempted to share the information and advice I have gathered in more than thirty years in this business. My hope is that it has demonstrated to retirees how they can breathe easier when they rely on a plan designed to provide income for life. It is clear that the three-legged stool of retirement is changing dramatically. Pensions, Social Security, and savings are no longer working in concert. More and more, it's a client's savings that is doing most of the work. Pensions are largely a thing of the past. Now most retirees have 401(k)s. And we know the implications associated with 401(k)s, chiefly that tax costs can drain them significantly. But there are alternatives and new opportunities to seize. With a financial plan that is balanced and working toward a goal, it is easier to take advantage of these new possibilities.

Just as athletes have a team of doctors and coaches they rely on for counsel, so too must the retiree seek advice from a team of professionals. Only then can the retiree address concerns and threats to his wealth. The primary threats include inflation, taxes, hidden fees in mutual funds, healthcare, and the long-term costs associated with living longer lives. We have covered these risks generally in this book, but when we actually plan for a client's retirement, each client receives extensive attention so as to offset unforeseen expenses and anticipate costs in the future.

In the end, it is my job to provide clients with the promise that they will be able to move forward into retirement with confidence, free of fear, so they and their heirs can enjoy a satisfying life.

Our motivation for doing what we do is not money; it is people. We try to instill the same idea when we advise clients. You make a plan not just to make sure you have income for life, but also for the people you care about, and the friends and family who make up your personal community. You want peace of mind for yourself, of course, but also for them. Our goal is to develop a financial plan that works for all involved. But clients must feel comfortable with what we present. It's the only way to be happy with the "Income Bliss" model. And that comfort depends on what type of investor you are.

One kind of investor is the delegator. The delegator is the ideal investor because he acquiesces to the advisor's expertise. When the delegator gives you his money, you get the chance to lay the groundwork for a successful plan right away. Assuming the advisor does a good job, the delegator receives a superior plan, because he has not inhibited the advisor's ability to manage.

Another kind of investor is the one who walks in with a plan in hand. It does not matter where the plan came from; he could have built it himself or purchased it from another firm. What matters is that when a client walks in with a plan and expects us to adhere to it—well, I hope you know by now, dear reader— that is not going to fly. Our plans typically do not seamlessly fold into plans made by other firms. It's because we're cautious, and we aim to secure income for life, not generate huge returns immediately. The investor who walks in with a plan usually walks out with a plan, but it's not by us.

Sometimes an investor looks to pit us against another firm, to see how we stand up. That is fine; people are free to compare us to any company they want. But the truth is, these investors usually do not wind up working with us. Why? Because I do not peddle fiction. I tell the investor exactly what we do and how we do it—that we are only interested in building plans that provide an income for life; that we do not work with thrill seek- ers looking to beat the market; and, most crucial of all, that we cannot deliver 5, 6, 7 percent returns for the next five years. The fact is, nobody can achieve those numbers, not consistently and predictably. But the other firm the investor is comparing us to usually claims that they can. So, the investor goes with them. Eventually, when he realizes he is not going to see those types of returns without taking on significant risks and thus putting the rest of his portfolio in jeopardy, he might come back to us and ask us to work with him. As we discussed in an earlier chapter, that only happens if the investor agrees to adhere to our plan. I am not in the business of people losing money.

Typically, those interested in massive short-term gains, the thrill seekers, do not have any interest in leaving a legacy. They have no skin in the game except their own. That is fine; it's their prerogative. But for us, we believe in working with the investors who have a desire to do good, and to leave the world a better place when they leave it. The longer I work in this business, the older I become, the more I believe in that. It's a driving principle of mine, these days, to acquire clients of the same temperament. I don't mean to sound exclusive to a fault; we will work with any person who shares our values. But if you do not have skin in the game, if you are not interested in generosity and warm-spiritedness, the fact is we do not have the time to engage your aspirations. Life is finite, and I want to do with it the very best that I can. I do not know when it will end, but I do know that I am going to do everything in my power to make opportunities to help people.

To me, the essential responsibility of an advisor, no matter if his advice is misguided, is taking the onus off the retiree. After all, the retiree has spent three-quarters of his life working. The fourth quarter should be spent enjoying his time. In my estimation, if you're up at night checking the market on your computer, anxious about how your assets are performing, it is not conducive to enjoying life, to relaxing and appreciating what you have accomplished. Our job as planners is to take the worries of the world, whether it is increasing interest rates, decreasing oil prices, fluctuating markets, or whatever the case may be, and sweep them into our briefcases. Let us worry about them. That's why you pay us. Remember, a good planner always pays for his fees. And while we cannot promise 10 percent returns, we can lower tax costs, create a lifetime income, and use the rest of the money for legacy planning. If we can use pennies to create dollars, we can free up more money to spend on other investments. We're planning for efficiency. Let us help you live your ideal life.

In closing, I'd like to offer a final reminder of why it is so important to seek professional advice when planning for retirement. With a financial plan in hand, you have peace of mind and direction. You feel confident about how much money you can spend and what you can do for others. In short, you feel enabled to pursue your dreams. Also, you are doing the right thing for your loved ones and the generations still to come.

You are faithful to your values and philosophies. By planning for the utmost efficiency, you will save money on taxes and other expenses and distribute the rest of your assets wisely. Most important of all, you are protecting all the years of hard work you put in, protecting those rewards for you and your loved ones.

Retirement planning is not easy, and it can be stressful. But I do not shirk from tough work, nor do I buckle under stress. In fact, with the "Income Bliss" model, we remove stress; we make the difficult questions easier to answer. It is always a pleasure to see a client enjoy his retirement free of financial worry.

For those who wish for the same kind of security and opportunity, be sure to seek professional advice. Better yet, visit me. We'll get to know each other. Heck, we may even make a plan for the future.

CASE STUDY: MITCH AND DEBBIE

MITCH AND DEBBIE WERE LIKE MANY OF OUR CLIents: they came to us after exhausting all the "traditional planning failures" used by most of the advisors in our industry. As I've said ad nauseam, many retirees fail due to using the same old planning strategies that were created to sell products rather than help folks retire with an income plan that will not die before they do.

Mitch and Debbie had good jobs, raised three great children in the Northeast, and endured the market corrections and the recessions of 2000-2002 and 2008-2009. At the end of 1999, they had amassed almost $2,000,000 in their brokerage accounts, IRAs, and 401(k)s. By the end of 2002, their accounts were almost all invested in stocks, mutual funds, exchange-traded funds, and selected bonds with a few REITs thrown in for good measure. They felt that life insurance was a rip-off. Well, they listened to all the talking heads on TV and talk radio—they bought term insurance and then dropped it after amassing $2 million. Heck, they were rich. No need for life insurance.

They had worked with their broker for fifteen years. He had explained to them that they could take systematic withdrawals from their portfolios and let the good times roll. He had told them over and over that a 5 percent withdrawal rate with a 3 percent inflation rate was a no-brainer and that (a) they would have a great lifestyle with a portfolio that was constantly growing, and (b) they would create a wonderful legacy for their children and grandchildren. This broker, however, had moved from wirehouse to wirehouse. As you might expect, his advice was unsound.

By the end of 2002, Mitch and Debbie's $2 million was worth $1.4 million. What's more, the only reason it wasn't less than that was primarily because Mitch had contributed more than $100,000 to IRAs and his 401(k) during that three-year period. Well, good news—their portfolio grew back to about $1.9 million by the summer of 2007. This, again, was partially due to the fact that Mitch was making the maximum contributions to his 401(k). Alas, by March 2009, their portfolio was down to $1.3 million. Finally, after screaming, begging, and pleading with their broker, they moved to an almost all-cash position and missed the March to December rebound of 2009.

Mitch and Debbie's story is a common tale. In the first quarter of 2010, they finally fired their broker, who, by the way, was still insistent that the "markets would right themselves" and Mitch and Debbie would be fine.

Mitch managed his own accounts for the balance of 2010. He then attended a dinner seminar and was introduced to a similar strategy as his previous broker's, only this time, variable annuities and managed accounts were substituted for mutual funds and stocks—really the same strategies used by his broker, just presented in a different wrapper. Mitch was cautious by now, actually paralyzed, and thankfully, he didn't tie up all his funds with big surrender charges and, once again, "live off the withdrawal opportunities." It was during this time that Mitch was referred to our group by one of his golf buddies—one of our happy clients.

So, Debbie and Mitch came to us in early 2011 with $1,260,000. They held in mind that their broker had all but assured them in early 2010 that they could easily withdraw $70,000 per year from their portfolio and never run out of money. He had said they could easily withdraw $100,000 per year when they had $2 million many years ago. Well, how did that work out?

I will not go through the planning process we did for them, as we have already covered the planning process earlier in the book, but needless to say, their original plans were not going to work.

AARP and other organizations have stated that even withdrawing 4 percent of your portfolio each year only has an 80 percent chance of working—that is, allowing you to have enough money for life—over the course of a thirty-year retirement. That equals $50,400 for Mitch and Debbie. Morningstar recommends an initial 2.8 percent withdrawal rate with 3 percent inflation increases, which results in an annual income of $35,280.00. How many ways can you say disappointing?

So, when Mitch turned sixty-six in April 2011 (Debbie is only two months younger), we "fixed" their plan. I am happy to say our plan has finally given them the peace of mind they were so longing for. In addition to their investments, Mitch and Debbie have Social Security checks and a $1,400 monthly pension that Mitch earned early in his career, back in the days when defined benefit plans were a normal employee perk.

Assets for Income Bliss Model (IBM)	
Total assets owned	$1,260,000—Starting point
Liquidity	$60,000—Left in checking account for the unknown
Fixed Index Annuity	$300,000—Lifetime income starting in year eight/LTC rider
SPIA—First seven years' income	$165,000—Income floor for years 1–7
SPIA for IUL Policy	$170,000—Insurance for income or death benefit
For IBM	$565,000—Left in Model (monthly income: age 100)

Balance Sheet for Mitch Income and Debbie Income

CASH ACCOUNTS

	Description	Owner	03/11/2018
☐	Checking	Joint	$60,000
Total cash accounts			**$60,000**

INVESTMENT ACCOUNTS

	Description	Owner	03/11/2018
☑	Brokerage	Joint	$320,000
☑	IRA	Mitch Income	$245,000
☐	SPIA for Life Policy	Mitch Income	$170,000
☐	Fixed Annuity Premium	Debbie Income	$300,000
☐	SPIA – 7 Years	Mitch Income	$165,000
Total investment accounts			**$1,200,000**

TOTAL AVAILABLE ASSETS	**$565,000**

INCOME SOURCES

	Description	Owner	Beginning Year	Ending Year	Inflation Rate	Annual Amount
A	Social Security	Mitch Income	2018	2052	1.00%	$30,480
B	Social Security	Debbie Income	2018	2052	1.00%	$21,120
C	Pension	Mitch Income	2018	2052	2.00%	$15,120
D	Income Assets IRA	Mitch Income	2018	2024	0.00%	$18,000
E	Annuity Income Rider IRA	Debbie Income	2025	2052	0.00%	$19,260
F	Life Insurance – 10 Pay	Mitch Income	2043	2053	0.00%	$40,000

Year	Age	Age	A	B	C	D	E	F	Total Base Income
2018	66	66	$30,480	$21,120	$15,120	$25,474	$0	$0	$92,194
2019	67	67	$30,785	$21,331	$15,422	$25,474	$0	$0	$93,012
2020	68	68	$31,093	$21,545	$15,731	$25,474	$0	$0	$93,842
2021	69	69	$31,404	$21,760	$16,045	$25,474	$0	$0	$94,683
2022	70	70	$31,718	$21,978	$16,366	$25,474	$0	$0	$95,536
2023	71	71	$32,035	$22,197	$16,694	$25,474	$0	$0	$96,400
2024	72	72	$32,355	$22,419	$17,028	$25,474	$0	$0	$97,276
2025	73	73	$32,679	$22,643	$17,368	$0	$19,260	$0	$91,950
2026	74	74	$33,005	$22,870	$17,715	$0	$19,260	$0	$92,851
2027	75	75	$33,336	$23,099	$18,070	$0	$19,260	$0	$93,764
2028	76	76	$33,669	$23,330	$18,431	$0	$19,260	$0	$94,690
2029	77	77	$34,006	$23,563	$18,800	$0	$19,260	$0	$95,628

2030	78	78	$34,346	$23,799	$19,176	$0	$19,260	$0	$96,580
2031	79	79	$34,689	$24,037	$19,559	$0	$19,260	$0	$97,545
2032	80	80	$35,036	$24,277	$19,951	$0	$19,260	$0	$98,523
2033	81	81	$35,386	$24,520	$20,350	$0	$19,260	$0	$99,516
2034	82	82	$35,740	$24,765	$20,757	$0	$19,260	$0	$100,522
2035	83	83	$36,098	$25,013	$21,172	$0	$19,260	$0	$101,542
2036	84	84	$36,459	$25,263	$21,595	$0	$19,260	$0	$102,576
2037	85	85	$36,823	$25,515	$22,027	$0	$19,260	$0	$103,625
2038	86	86	$37,191	$25,770	$22,468	$0	$19,260	$0	$104,689
2039	87	87	$37,563	$26,028	$22,917	$0	$19,260	$0	$105,768
2040	88	88	$37,939	$26,288	$23,375	$0	$19,260	$0	$106,863
2041	89	89	$38,318	$26,551	$23,843	$0	$19,260	$0	$107,972
2042	90	90	$38,702	$26,817	$24,320	$0	$19,260	$0	$109,098
2043	91	91	$39,089	$27,085	$24,806	$0	$19,260	$40,000	$150,239
2044	92	92	$39,479	$27,356	$25,302	$0	$19,260	$40,000	$151,397
2045	93	93	$39,874	$27,629	$25,808	$0	$19,260	$40,000	$152,572
2046	94	94	$40,273	$27,906	$26,324	$0	$19,260	$40,000	$153,763
2047	95	95	$40,676	$28,185	$26,851	$0	$19,260	$40,000	$154,971
2048	96	96	$41,082	$28,467	$27,388	$0	$19,260	$40,000	$156,197
2049	97	97	$41,493	$28,751	$27,936	$0	$19,260	$40,000	$157,440
2050	98	98	$41,908	$29,039	$28,494	$0	$19,260	$40,000	$158,701
2051	99	99	$42,327	$29,329	$29,064	$0	$19,260	$40,000	$159,981
2052	100	100	$42,751	$29,622	$29,645	$0	$19,260	$40,000	$161,278
2053	101	101	$0	$0	$0	$0	$0	$40,000	$40,000

Note: Income Sources data are based on information provided by you (the client). If this information is incorrect, the illustration will not be valid. These values are based on hypothetical inflation assumptions. These values are not representative of an actual investment; should not be considered a projection of future performance; and are provided for illustrative purposes only. There is no guarantee that any investment strategy will meet its stated objectives.

SCENARIO ILLUSTRATION

The total current assets available for use (listed on the balance sheet) are divided among these hypothetical portfolios, each with various hypothetical rates of return given your (the client's) particular financial need and expected time frame. Each portfolio has two corresponding columns in the table below showing the proposed growth and distribution of assets from that particular portfolio.

Desired Annual Income before Taxes	$90,000
Income Inflation Rate	3.00%
Fixes Rate	2.00%
Income Plan Duration	35 years

The scenario is currently using $565,000 of the $565,000 in available assets.

Under this current income plan, you will have $714,219 remaining at the age of 100.

Portfolio 1: $10,348 (2%)

Duration: 5 years
Growth Rate: 2.00%

Portfolio 2: $63,893 (11%)

Duration: 5 years
Growth Rate: 4.00%

Portfolio 3: $244,577 (43%)

Duration: 5 years
Growth Rate: 6.00%

Portfolio 4: $246,182 (44%)

Duration: 5 years
Growth Rate: 6.00%

			Portfolio 1		Portfolio 2		Portfolio 3		Portfolio 4					
Year	Age		Growth @ 2%	Fixed @ 2%	Growth @ 4%	Fixed @ 2%	Growth @ 6%	Fixed @ 2%	Growth @ 6%	Fixed @ 2%	Other Income	Portfolio Income	Total Annual Income	Total Portfolio Assets
2018	66	66		$10,348	$63,893		$244,577		$246,182		$92,194	$0	$90,000	$512,100
2019	67	67		$10,555	$66,449		$259,252		$260,953		$93,012	$0	$92,700	$534,168
2020	68	68		$10,766	$69,107		$274,807		$276,610		$93,842	$1,639	$95,481	$555,760
2021	69	69		$9,310	$71,871		$291,295		$293,207		$94,683	$3,662	$98,345	$576,855
2022	70	70		$5,760	$74,746		$308,773		$310,799		$95,536	$5,760	$101,296	$597,432
2023	71	71				$77,736	$327,299		$329,447		$96,400	$7,935	$104,335	$734,482
2024	72	72				$71,197	$346,937		$349,214		$97,276	$10,189	$107,465	$767,348
2025	73	73				$62,229	$367,753		$370,167		$91,950	$18,738	$110,689	$800,149
2026	74	74				$44,360	$389,818		$392,377		$92,851	$21,158	$114,009	$826,555
2027	75	75				$23,666	$413,208		$415,920		$93,764	$23,666	$117,430	$852,793
2028	76	76					$285,475	$152,526	$440,875		$94,690	$26,263	$120,952	$878,875
2029	77	77					$302,603	$128,788	$467,327		$95,628	$28,953	$124,581	$898,718
2030	78	78					$320,759	$101,832	$495,367		$96,580	$31,738	$128,318	$917,958
2031	79	79					$340,005	$71,495	$525,089		$97,545	$34,623	$132,168	$936,589
2032	80	80					$360,405	$37,610	$556,594		$98,523	$37,610	$136,133	$954,609

Year													
2033	81	81				$382,029		$363,081	$226,909	$99,516	$40,702	$140,217	$972,019
2034	82	82				$404,951		$384,866	$189,931	$100,522	$43,902	$144,424	$979,748
2035	83	83				$429,248		$407,958	$148,950	$101,542	$47,215	$148,756	$986,156
2036	84	84				$455,003		$432,435	$103,770	$102,576	$50,643	$153,219	$991,208
2037	85	85				$482,303		$458,381	$54,190	$103,625	$54,190	$157,816	$994,875
2038	86	86				$196,029	$315,212	$485,884		$104,689	$57,861	$162,550	$997,126
2039	87	87				$207,791	$262,499	$515,037		$105,768	$61,658	$167,427	$985,327
2040	88	88				$220,258	$204,857	$545,939		$106,863	$65,587	$172,449	$971,055
2041	89	89				$233,474	$142,056	$578,696		$107,972	$69,650	$177,623	$954,225
2042	90	90				$247,482	$73,854	$613,418		$109,098	$73,854	$182,951	$934,753
2043	91	91				$262,331		$422,745	$227,478	$150,239	$38,201	$188,440	$912,554
2044	92	92				$278,071		$448,110	$193,063	$151,397	$42,696	$194,093	$919,243
2045	93	93				$294,755		$474,996	$153,374	$152,572	$47,344	$199,916	$923,126
2046	94	94				$312,441		$503,496	$108,150	$153,763	$52,151	$205,913	$924,087
2047	95	95				$331,187		$533,706	$57,120	$154,971	$57,120	$212,091	$922,012
2048	96	96					$351,058	$565,728		$156,197	$62,257	$218,454	$916,786
2049	97	97					$294,577	$599,672		$157,440	$67,567	$225,007	$894,249
2050	98	98					$231,550	$635,652		$158,701	$73,056	$231,757	$867,203
2051	99	99					$161,664	$673,791		$159,981	$78,730	$238,710	$835,455
2052	100	100					$84,593	$714,219		$161,278	$84,593	$245,871	$798,812
Totals								$714,219		$4,023,185	$1,420,909	$5,444,094	$714,219

Note: Scenario Illustration data is based on information provided by you (the client). If this information is incorrect, the illustration will not be valid. Portfolio withdrawals are based on the strategy illustration outlined on this page and is based on hypothetical rates of return and inflation assumptions. These values are not representative of an actual investment; should not be considered a projection of future performance; and are provided for illustrative purposes only. All investments involve risk. There is no guarantee that any investment strategy will meet its stated objectives. This page illustrates the proposed allocation of your accounts to the various buckets. This is not intended to propose a specific investment, only facilitate a discussion with your financial advisor in determining the appropriate allocation strategy for each account. Higher rates of return are typically associated with greater risk and potential loss of principal.

The previous example of an "Income Bliss" model illustrates how money is allocated, where it goes over time, and what to expect in terms of returns. If you review it carefully, you will see the math is correct and it truly delivers what it promises.

I encourage you to heed the lessons in this book. They will make a big difference to your retirement's health, both financially and emotionally. If you have questions or comments, please feel free to get in touch with me by visiting my firm's website: www.wsgadvisors.com.

ACKNOWLEDGEMENTS

Writing a book is hard, sort of like building a house: the first part goes smoothly and easy, you can see the progress, but as you get closer to the finished product, it's like the meticulous finish work in completing a new home.

I have had the pleasure of working with many great people in my thirty-plus years in this rewarding business, and while it would be impossible to acknowledge everyone that I have learned from through the years, several stand out to me. David Macchia, developer of The Income for Life Model, and Stephen Swensen, president of Bucket Bliss, have had a profound effect on the evolution of our planning processes. Don Blanton, MoneyTrax; Len Renier, founder of Wealth *&* Wisdom; Matt Zagula, developer of SMART Retirement; and the gentleman who coaxed me into this great business over thirty-five years ago—Terry Keiper. They all had a hand in this manuscript in some way.

ABOUT THE AUTHOR

Bob Gardner, CLU, ChFC, RFC, has been a practicing financial advisor for more than three decades. As president of WSG Advisors, Bob focuses his expertise on comprehensive wealth management for retirees and pre-retirees. With a strong background in financial services and insurance, Bob has knowledge of how money works and, more importantly, how to make it work for his clients. Since his college days, he has continually worked to further his professional education and business acumen. Committed to helping retirees and pre-retirees live their ideal lives, Bob has conducted more than 320 seminars and workshops since 1997, as well as more than 4,000 consulting interviews with individuals in or nearing retirement. A native South Carolinian, Bob and his family have been residents of Hilton Head Island since 2004.

www.ingramcontent.com/pod-product-compliance
Lightning Source LLC
Chambersburg PA
CBHW022207050726
47590CB00002B/687